"This book is many things: a harrowingly frank, first-hand account of surviving debilitating mental illness; a thoughtful and complex effort to integrate and synthesize the languages of theology and psychiatry; an artful attempt to offer sympathy and spiritual sustenance to fellow sufferers. But it is, more than anything else, a hymn of love and longing for Jesus, the living Lord who will not break a bruised reed or snuff out a dimly burning wick."

Wesley Hill,
associate professor of New Testament,
Western Theological Seminary, Holland, MI

"Our lives are not tidy nor are our personal stories always a cheery 'upward and onward' narrative. Instead, we often face deep valleys with frightening darkness and endless unknowns. John A. Bryant's book is not 'tidy' either, but because of his experience with and honesty about mental illness and trauma, we can learn from him; more importantly, because he points us to Christ crucified, we have more than a story, we have hope."

Kelly M. Kapic,
author of *You're Only Human* and *Embodied Hope*

"Theology is often merely academic, done for its own sake in the hallowed halls of sacred academies. And struggles with mental illness are often kept hidden from the public, endured by the one suffering from it and shared only with family, friends and therapists. John Bryant has chosen to be both fully transparent about his struggles with mental illness and also address the challenges theologically in a way that is utterly transparent, in the open for all to see and with a sensitivity that will encourage all who read *A Quiet Mind to Suffer With*. This book will make you weep, enlarge your empathy, and, Lord willing, instill a compassion in you for the mentally ill. Please do not merely read this text but understand it as an invitation into the wounds of Christ that gives meaning to all suffering."

Greg Peters,
Biola University and Nashotah House Theological Seminary;
author of *Monkhood of All Believers*

"This is a stunning book, so rare and so beautiful. I cannot recommend it highly enough. John Bryant does two things that are very hard to do at the same time. He represents the raw agony and disorientation of healing from OCD. And he puts this struggle within a hopeful theological frame. I cried a lot during this book. It will encourage those who suffer and help others to understand the struggle. The book is honest, vulnerable, gripping, and hopeful at the same time. Read this book."

Matthew A. LaPine,
director of Christian education at Citylight Church in Omaha, NE;
author of *The Logic of the Body*

"It is perhaps one of the great ironies of our therapeutic age that our dependence upon said therapy from time to time does not free us but binds us all the more to our problems. With his Christocentric focus, John Bryant offers a much-needed corrective to our profound difficulties. Perhaps most importantly, he offers hope when our deepest problems are not 'fixed' and a reminder of our Lord's promise that his grace is sufficient for us all (2 Corinthians 12:9)."

Philip Jamieson,
author of *The Face of Forgiveness: A Pastoral Theology of Shame and Redemption*

"In these days when we are seeking thrills and 'image is everything,' John goes to a place where few dare to tread, into his, and our, soul. Setting aside the distractions of this world, John examines the reality of human suffering as he has experienced it. In so doing, the sand of his discomfort has produced a beautiful pearl in the form of his book. In truth, we all suffer from mental trauma to one degree or another. John's book helps us to examine those traumas and find healing. Perhaps an irony of John's inner analysis is that his contemplative nature makes him an excellent social activist. He understands people where they live, below the surface, behind the image. Church Army USA is blessed to have him working for us as he serves Christ and loves hurting people."

Greg Miller,
executive director, Church Army USA

"John is an artist who builds for the reader an interior world with its own cast of characters and a logic all its own. He takes readers on a poetic journey through mental suffering, and he holds his experience up to the light, turning it over and over, so we get a glimpse of it from every angle, observing how the divine and mundane interact. We come away knowing that the divine is what's real after all. And while this story is deeply personal and utterly unique, he gives the reader enough so that they can say, 'Me too,' even as it inspires in the reader a compassion for someone struggling with darker demons. No matter what, the practice is the same: Christ, have mercy. It must all be an offering."

Pamela Rossi-Keen, PhD, PMP,
executive director, The Genesis Collective

"In *A Quiet Mind to Suffer With*, John Bryant shows us his full self, and in turn we see our own reflections as 'wounded selfish people ... uninterpretable to others and a deep mystery to ourselves.' Like Bryant, we long to learn 'to become a patient, quiet man who is headed somewhere.' In our contemporary world, this longing can prove quite difficult, and perhaps can only be achieved—for some of us—through painful struggle. This book offers a way to find our own peculiar stance in this world, our own solid ground on which to stand, and ultimately, it offers us a quiet place of our own."

Glenn Taylor,
author of *The Marrowbone Marble Company*

"John Bryant's life is a powerful and fitting testament to the intricacy and fraught nature of our individual and shared humanity. He enters the chasm of mental illness with courage and remains there so that we all may experience the natural ways of healing once we journey together into vulnerability. I'm struck by the notion that whatever our ego speaks, we must not be afraid in the end to eat our own humiliation and prepare for what the divine mysteries of God may have waiting. There is a vessel of light in the abyss. We rise as if on angels' wings, returning to greater human touch, love, and existence as we find ourselves, as John did, 'welcomed back into the tenderness and frailty' of life, 'in awe' not only because of the fear we've encountered but also due to a new vision of 'thanksgiving and grace.' "

Shann Ray,
author of *American Masculine*, *American Copper*, *Atomic Theory 432*, *Balefire*, *Sweetclover*, and *Forgiveness and Power in the Age of Atrocity*

"John has crafted a powerful, personal, and poignant account of intimacy with the real Jesus: a trusted friend who walks with weary transgressors through banal, bleak, and sorrowful landscapes. His writing offers a simple and steady life of worship as a spiritual balm for those with wounded minds."

Jake Rozmus,
singer/songwriter in Burgettstown, PA

"Few things catalyze tears to fall freely from my eyes, but this book did that very thing. If you've wondered how dark, seemingly irredeemable pain can fit in Christ's plan for your life, this book is for you. We all want to know what 'getting better' looks like, and John prayerfully gives a faithful answer to that question. I can attest that the framework being presented in this book is not just an esoteric brain exercise—John really depends on Christ, and that encourages me to become a little more needy also."

Andrew Tyson,
singer/songwriter in Nashville, TN;
frontman of pop-punk band Real Face

"In these pages we meet a writer, a comedian, a victim of mental illness, a great sufferer, and, above all, one who has known the astounding mercy of Christ. John takes us through the doors of trauma and tragedy straight into the heart of this mercy, down to its bottomless depths. His story, so important for the church to hear, reminds us who Christ is: God with us, even in hell. And even in hell, our hope."

Deanna Briody,
poet, writer, and postulant for Holy Orders in the Episcopal Church

"*A Quiet Mind to Suffer With* is nothing less than a deeply personal and relevant vindication of the gospel's undying power to reach into our anxious and distracted age, to slow us down and show us mercy, and to so shepherd our memories that we might, all of us, begin to feel the warmth of hope once more."

Clint Wilson,
community and care pastor of City Church Houston, Houston, TX

"Until Christ comes again, the Christian lives in the strange country between the inauguration of the kingdom of God and its perfect fulfillment. John's memoir plots a course through this foreign landscape—complete with a strange, insightful new language—that provides resources for those brutal moments in which God chooses not to heal us in the way we would like, in order that He might make us whole by different means. John struggles with a mental illness, but his story offers hope to those struggling with doubt, with pain, and with Jesus in it all. It offers hope to me."

Drew Miller,
assistant rector of St. John's Church, Florence, SC

"*A Quiet Mind to Suffer With* is a theological exploration of what mental illness feels like from the inside. Written with the irreverent candor of Francis Spufford and the pastoral sensitivity of Henri Nouwen, it's for those who don't make sense to themselves and for those trying to walk alongside them. John is, by no means, alone in his experience, but I do believe he is alone in his ability to tell us about it. You will want to read it in one sitting and give it away to someone else."

Austin Gohn,
author of *A Restless Age*;
lead pastor of Bellevue Christian Church, Bellevue, PA

"While I don't have OCD, I do have a brain that is always struggling with figuring out, knowing for sure, defending myself, and trying to make things right. John Bryant's *A Quiet Mind to Suffer With* is a gift to those, like me, that can't turn off their thoughts and need a Word for the present time of suffering. What I love about John is that he has the credibility to proclaim the good news in the darkest of places and grace in the most mundane of habits. I am looking forward to sharing this with many of my parishioners, friends, and family that pray for a quiet mind."

Luke Deman,
rector of St. Timothy's Anglican Church, Summerville, SC

"This book is oxygen for those desperate for air. John's ability to share his own pain and trauma in a way that reveals the Savior who bears our trauma is a much-needed witness for Christians who suffer in silence."

Caleb Musselman,
pastor of Soma Church, Beaver Falls, PA

"Part essay, part sermon, part narrative poem, this book ministers to the clinically anxious. Bryant's message is grounded in the Gospel and honed through daily practice of what he preaches."

Austin Freeman,
author of *Tolkien Dogmatics:*
Theology through Mythology with the Maker of Middle-Earth

A QUIET MIND TO SUFFER WITH

Mental Illness, Trauma, and the Death of Christ

A QUIET MIND TO SUFFER WITH

Mental Illness, Trauma, and the Death of Christ

JOHN ANDREW BRYANT

LEXHAM PRESS

A Quiet Mind to Suffer With: Mental Illness, Trauma, and the Death of Christ

Lexham Press, 1313 Commercial St., Bellingham, WA 98225
LexhamPress.com

Print ISBN 9781683597049
Digital ISBN 9781683597056
Library of Congress Control Number 2023930830

Lexham Editorial: Todd Hains, Jeff Reimer, Mandi Newell, Jessi Strong
Cover Design: Joshua Hunt
Typesetting: Abigail Stocker

CONTENTS

GLOSSARY OF TERMS

THE SIREN: the word for a mental illness, specifically obsessive-compulsive disorder. Also referred to as My Affliction, What's Wrong, the Bully, the Accuser, and What Should Happen. A word for the mind's painful, powerful intimidation.

THE REALM OF CEASELESS COGNITION: a term for excessive rumination, the network of compulsions that serve as a way to deal with the Siren. The four primary ones: figuring out, knowing for sure, defending myself, making things right. Also known as the Haunted House.

THE HARDNESS OF THE HEART: a term for my addiction to my dependence on myself. Also referred to as Sin and Life as I Would Have It and What I'll Do to Be Okay. A blindness we cannot seem to get rid of.

A BODY THAT EXPECTS THE WORLD TO END: another term for trauma. Also referred to as What Could Happen, the way the Past lives in the body. A word for the body's cringing, crying anticipation.

THE HOWLING BOY: a term for the soul's anguish, despair, and unbearable dissatisfaction. The Howling Boy is the soul that has suffered History and Affliction, OCD and trauma.

PATIENT, QUIET UNDERSTANDING: a term for humility, and the trust I have in Christ.

THE WILDERNESS OF HISTORY AND AFFLICTION: a term for the present time of Suffering. The world we live in. A world where anything can be seen, felt, done, or taken. Also known as What's Wrong and What Happened.

THE WORD: the gospel, the news that Christ has died and Christ has risen and Christ will come again, the forgiveness of sin.

THE RHYTHM: a simple life of hearing, prayer, and offering, where our trust is rescued, led, and fulfilled. Also known as an Ordinary Life of Regular Worship. The relationship everyday life has to Christ's death, resurrection, and return.

THE STRANGERS: the word for what body, mind, and soul become to us when we suffer. Also referred to as the John Who Feels This Way.

A PRAYER IN THE WILDERNESS OF A MENTAL ILLNESS

In the Name of the Father and of the + Son and of the Holy Spirit. Amen.

Out of the deep have I called unto you, O LORD; *
    Lord, hear my voice.
O let your ears consider well *
    the voice of my supplications.
If you, LORD, were to mark what is done amiss, *
    O Lord, who could abide it?
For there is mercy with you; *
    therefore you shall be feared.
I wait for the LORD; my soul waits for him; *
    in his word is my trust.
My soul waits for the Lord, *
    more than watchmen for the morning,
    more than watchmen for the morning.
O Israel, trust in the LORD, for with the LORD there is mercy, *
    and with him is plenteous redemption;
And he shall redeem Israel *
    from all their sins.

Psalm 130

Glory be to the Father and to the Son and to the Holy Spirit; *
as it was in the beginning, is now, and ever shall be,
world without end. Amen.

Lord, have mercy on us.
Christ, have mercy on us.
Lord, have mercy on us.

Our Father, who art in heaven,
hallowed be thy name.
Thy kingdom come.
Thy will be done, on earth as it is in heaven.
Give us this day our daily bread.
And forgive us our trespasses,
as we forgive those who trespass against us.
And lead us not into temptation,
but deliver us from evil. *Matthew 6:9–13*
For thine is the kingdom and the glory and the power
forever and ever.
Amen.

FOREWORD

Kathryn Greene-McCreight

PEOPLE AFFLICTED WITH MENTAL ILLNESSES may experience the same symptoms but manage them differently. This is because, while symptoms are outwardly expressed, they are also inwardly experienced. The signs and symptoms themselves are identifiable: my son will not get out of bed; my daughter hears voices that others do not hear; my minister has fits of rage for no apparent reason. These symptoms are organized into discrete diagnoses of diseases, each appearing as a code in the *Diagnostic and Statistical Manual of Mental Disorders* for insurance and medication purposes. But each person responds to symptoms and manages them in their own unique ways.

How we experience these symptoms inwardly also differs from person to person. Her symptoms cause her feelings of shame or self-hatred; his symptoms cause him anger and guilt; for another all of these are present at once, or not at all. How we react to these various feelings and experiences forms yet another layer of complication. One person cannot bear to be perceived as sick, so they expend a lot of energy trying to seem fine; another feels her church must not know she is ill and retreats into silent absence. One person tries to shelter others from themselves; another wants to blame others.

Muddying matters further is the question of how other people (family and friends and colleagues) react to the individual's affliction. Does her sense of shame at her own symptoms appear to her family as a rejection of them? How do they react to this? Does his raging cause his parishioners to blame themselves? How do they take on this anger in their own interactions with him? Supporting others in times of mental affliction requires acknowledging all of these layers.

If we take seriously these complex layers of mental illness, mental health is how we live our lives oriented toward the good. John Bryant points to this. The problem is not so much the thoughts and the feelings created by his disease, but how he tries to manage them, what he does with them. He learns to offer up these thoughts and feelings to Christ and to depend on His Mercy—rather than himself—to be enough to sustain and lead him.

John confronts his reader with important questions: "But who is Christ? And who am I? Where am I going? And what am I supposed to be doing?" He shows how these questions, key for any Christian, can become cruel taunts for those who are afflicted by mental illnesses. Depression, anxiety, schizoaffective disorder (to name but a few) muffle the questions and block healthy responses to them. Shame, dread, fear, emptiness, and isolation threaten to veil the Lord's presence from the believer.

The term "recovery" seems a chimera, a mocking insult. There is no recovery, and all of life is reduced to a Sisyphusian attempt to bear the crushing weight of the cross, with no sign of hope or hint of the empty tomb. John speaks with courageous vulnerability into this tangle of issues as one who trusts Christ even in the misery of affliction.

> How long, O LORD? Will you forget me forever?
> How long will you hide your face from me?
> How long must I take counsel in my soul
> and have sorrow in my heart all the day?
> How long shall my enemy be exalted over me?
> But I have trusted in your steadfast love;
> my heart shall rejoice in your salvation.
> I will sing to the LORD,
> because he has dealt bountifully with me.
>
> *Psalm 13:1–2, 5–6*

WE PROCLAIM THE MYSTERY OF OUR FAITH

The Word, the Way, and the Amen

PART I

WORD AND UNDERSTANDING

MY THOUGHTS ARE GEMS AND BASTARDS, but it's a stretch to say they're mine. With thoughts this vivid, uncontrolled, and catastrophic, I am rather, it seems, at their mercy. If they are mine, they are only mine in this way: that I am the one they are happening to. I am the one who has to see them.

I live like a lot of people. I see people, I do things. I eat cereal, I drive a truck, and I try to be kind. But with a brain that sends me nightmares during the day—thoughts parading down the hall of my mind, vivid images both bizarre and impossible, at various turns random, sexual, violent—I've had to come to terms with the fact that I have a brain that says what I don't mean and shows me what I don't want to see: horrible things to look at while I'm trying to work and eat and live.

In the psychiatric community they are called intrusive thoughts.

I have also had to come to terms with the fact that I have a brain that—along with saying what I don't mean, and showing me what I don't want to see—makes me feel what I don't understand. Incredible and overwhelming verdicts of shame, fear, and dread—dark and horrible feelings so shattering and conclusive they could only be overturned by the death of the Son of God.

By my brain I have been made to see and feel horrors, have lived, in particular, under the vicious regime of three dark and horrible feelings my whole life, with a brain that says

Something is wrong (shame).

Something is intolerable (dread).

Something bad is going to happen (fear).

In light of those bizarre thoughts and those awful feelings that it has created, my brain then tells me What Should Happen, handing out its two commands:

You need to do something to be okay.

You have to have something to be okay.

I have learned to refer to those bizarre and awful thoughts, those three powerful feelings, and those two bizarre commands, collectively, as the Siren. I also know it, affectionately, as My Affliction and What's Wrong With My Brain.

In the psychiatric community, it is known as obsessive-compulsive disorder.

The Siren is my word for the intensity and pull of a mental illness. For me it has a double meaning: the Siren refers both to a car alarm going off and the creatures that tried to pull Odysseus into the rocks by singing to him. It is both urgency and urge, both warning and command, both scream and pull, both obsession and compulsion.

The Siren is my word for the fact that the world is not what my brain says it is. It is a word that has helped me live with the fact that my brain is not my friend. It is a word that has helped me not be devoured by the symptoms of a mental illness.

Those dark and awful thoughts and feelings are, the brain scans have shown, just chemicals in the brain misfiring. I have a brain unlike other brains. It consistently and persuasively misinforms. It is always telling me things that are not true.

Those dark and awful thoughts and feelings, however, are not received as data or information, or even misinformation, but are consistently experienced as gods, as omens, as verdicts, and as dark prophetic utterances. They make their appearance in my life as the Final Word and the End of the World. The final Word on life, the final Word on others, the final Word on myself.

And so I have also learned to call the Siren not only My Affliction or What's Wrong but also the Bully and the Accuser.

People with obsessive-compulsive disorder, when met with the horrible things their brain can show them, and just how bad their brain can make them feel, do things to make their brain stop screaming at them. They obey its command so it will leave them alone.

That is, faced with those obsessions (those distressing thoughts and feelings, what their brain says is wrong, or intolerable, or about to happen), they give in to compulsions (what the brain says has to happen) so they will feel okay.

They scrub floors; they check things. They create magic numbers or habits to dampen or avoid the verdict their brain has provided, the verdict that says life is intolerable and unbearable, that something is absolutely, excruciatingly wrong, that something absolutely must be done, that something must be fixed. They do this to console themselves. They do this so they'll be okay.

My compulsion, my urge, is to go into my head and do four things: figure out, know for sure, defend myself, and make things right. My compulsion is excessive rumination. Over the last thirty years, this compulsion has formed into an immense, labyrinthine, tangled, trapdoor mansion located only in my head: a tangled nest of circuits, a constant and looping embroidery of thoughts to mitigate, satisfy, outrun, and overturn the verdicts handed down by the Siren, the horrors I can be made to see and feel if I don't think better and think more. I have learned to call this constant, looping embroidery of thoughts, this vast network of compulsions, the Realm of Ceaseless Cognition. I will also call it the Haunted House. That is what it felt like over the years. This tangled network of compulsions has felt like a Haunted House.

The Realm of Ceaseless Cognition is the place I go to check and make sure, the place I go to defend myself against cataclysm and defamation, the place I go to figure things out and make things right when the Siren says something is wrong (and something is always wrong). It is the place where I go to know for sure nothing bad will happen when the Siren tells me something bad is about to happen. The Haunted House is where I go to hide from all the things the Siren says cannot be tolerated, where I go to hide from what I can be made to see and what I can be made to feel.

The Realm of Ceaseless Cognition has been the country I have lived in all my life, the world I've been in instead of being in the world. The Haunted House is the place where I have learned to go and depend on myself. It is where my dependence on myself has taken root, where it has been deepened, honored, cultivated, satisfied, and become its own stronghold, its own place. This vast network of cognition and self-deception is my place of enslavement. It is where I am misshapen. And it has made my life lonely in ways I do not know how to explain to the people I love most.

THIS MEMOIR IS ABOUT HOW I learned to leave that place, the Haunted House, the Realm of Ceaseless Cognition, that immense, tangled mass of hypervigilant rumination that I once thought was the same thing as myself. It is how I learned to leave my own shadow. And how I learned to move in the opposite direction of the greatest perceived needs of my life: the need to figure things out so I will be okay, the need to know for sure so I will be okay, the need to defend myself so I will be okay, the need to go into my head and make things right so I will be okay.

It's the story of how I left the Realm of Ceaseless Cognition and began to be quietly changed by heading somewhere else.

But it is not the story of how I got rid of a mental illness by believing in Jesus.

I have not, in getting better, removed this illness or its symptoms. The Siren I've stopped worshiping is still there. The warnings and commands still go off like missiles and fireworks, and savagely strike both mind and heart. And recovery has not meant making that go away, has not meant policing the appearance of those dark and awful thoughts, or mitigating the intensity and pull of those dark and awful feelings. They are still very real and very painful to me. They are still the experience provided by my brain.

It has been important for me over the years to not understand a mental illness as a character flaw or a lack of faith when it is simply an Affliction, a kind of Suffering among other kinds of Suffering. I simply have a brain that provides horrors to be seen and felt. I have a brain that provides great anguish and distress without any warning and without my volition. A mental illness, of course, is affected by and related to many other things in life, but it is most simply just that: an experience provided by the brain.

I love Jesus and am still very much mentally ill. My love for Jesus has not fixed that. And Jesus' love for me has not fixed it either. I love Jesus very, very much. And I've still been made to see and feel horrors.

The Siren is still there, wailing, lying, bullying, intimidating. Still there, still so swaggering and urgent and full of itself, pumping my body with dumbstruck, awe-filled dread, always coming up with something dark and horrible for me to be afraid of or look at. The only difference now is that those symptoms are a Wilderness I walk through rather than a god I worship.

The Siren has not gone. It is only our relationship that has changed. It is only that I have learned to stop worshiping It.

I have not, as of yet, been rescued either by therapy or medication from the intensity and appearance of those thoughts and feelings, that scream and pull, those warnings and commands, but only from the trust I had in them. And I have spent the last three years learning that it is only the thoughts and feelings we trust that get to kill us, that the saddest thing in the world isn't to have bad thoughts or feelings. The saddest thing in the world is to believe things that are not true.

That is what recovery has meant for me.

And it looks like this: to walk down the street, or drive my car, or be sitting with my wife, and

To think that something is wrong.

And to feel like something is wrong.

And to understand nothing is wrong.

This may not be what other people mean by recovery. But that is what I mean. For as long as I can remember, my life has been a stalemate between how I feel, what I think, and what I understand. And now I know that what I understand will always mean more than what I can be made to think and feel by the faulty wiring in my brain. That understanding has, and will, determine more of the course of my life than this bewildering Affliction.

I don't need to have the right thoughts and the right feelings to be okay. That is what I understand now. And while those thoughts and feelings can riot and rage, while they can fluctuate in intensity and fling out their own provocative new content, the patient, quiet understanding that I am already okay can still deepen. I can understand I'm okay when I don't feel okay. And with that understanding I can walk through the Wilderness of those bewildering symptoms and have myself a little life. With that understanding I can patiently endure what can be seen and felt. I can patiently endure these horrors I've been made to see and feel.

It turns out that patient, quiet understanding is the only thing I need to be okay. And it turns out the world changes shape around what I understand. It can turn a terrifying god into a simple Wilderness. It can turn a bully into symptoms. This understanding has been the chief Mercy of my life. And Mercy, I've learned, is not a feeling that must be felt, or thought that we must think, but a Reality that is understood.

For the longest time I thought I was the symptoms of my illness, that I was as dark and horrible as they were. That I was the same as what my brain did, the same as what it showed me. But now I know those thoughts and feelings are mine only in the sense that I am the one they're happening to, the one in the Wilderness of what I can be made to see and feel. I'm just the one making my way through what my mind can show me.

When my mind became a terrifying, threatening Stranger, when all normal thoughts and feelings were taken from me, it seemed all I had was that understanding. The understanding that I was okay. And since that understanding was all I had, I decided that understanding was who I was.

Rather than those thoughts, or my feelings, I seem to have become that patient, quiet understanding. I have become, instead of my thoughts and feelings, a hard kernel of patient, quiet trust.

A patient, quiet understanding that is simply my ability to trust. An understanding of the heart.

And I count that patient, quiet understanding—that hard kernel of patient quiet trust—as more dearly bought and more vigilantly guarded than anything else in my life. It has been more precious to me than better thoughts, and better feelings. I make my way through the Wilderness of what can be thought and what can be felt as that patient, quiet understanding, a sojourner in the Wilderness of the experiences created by my mind.

It has also, at times, felt like being a small, unsinkable boat in a great storm. A storm no one else can see because it is, as they say, all in your head.

That understanding, that small boat, that hard kernel of patient, quiet trust has a uniquely religious valence. It is the patient, quiet trust I have in Christ. It is the patient, quiet understanding of who Christ is. A capacity to quietly hand myself over to who I know Christ to be and to know I am okay.

This is not, of course, what I wanted. What I wanted was better thoughts and better feelings. The absence of Suffering. I wanted my brain to provide better experiences. And what I got was a better understanding of who Christ is and who I am; where I'm headed and what I'm supposed to be doing.

The word "understanding" may be tricky. It may take some time to know what I mean by it, but what I mean by it is what Scripture means by humility, reverence, and the fear of the Lord. An understanding of the heart. A posture, a way to live by faith. A humility that is not a command or a feeling but a gift and an inheritance, the condition of knowing who Christ is so that I know who we are, so that we know where we're going, and what we're supposed to be doing.

The heart is not a thought or feeling but our capacity to trust, to hand ourselves over to what is trusted. We cannot see or even really feel this "heart." But it is the heart that consecrates everything we can see and feel.

What do I need to be okay? The Siren would say the only thing I need to be okay is to obey its warnings and commands. But it turns out the only thing I need to be okay is to know who Christ is and who I am, where I'm going and what I'm supposed to be doing. That humility, that understanding, is all I need to leave the Haunted House of compulsions and make my way through the Wilderness of bewildering symptoms.

But who is Christ? And who am I? Where am I going? And what am I supposed to be doing?

It is something I ask myself and I have learned to tell myself simply, that Christ is the Mercy that has been offered, that I am servant and guest of the Mercy that has been offered, that I am headed into the future provided by the Mercy that has been offered, and that, until it arrives, the only thing I can really do is behold, be patient, and bear witness to the Mercy that has been offered.

I am not the Mercy that has been offered. I have not died for the sins of the world. Neither have you. But I can understand that Mercy has been offered. And I can become that understanding. It has been an agony to have to become something so simple. It is like being winnowed down to a single hot coal that cannot be put out. It is like falling down a mountain until you find a single place to put your foot and stand. Because it is felt so simply it is felt more deeply and more powerfully. And the deeper the understanding, the quieter I have become. Especially in turmoil, and even in great anguish and distress.

None of the horrors I have been made to think or feel have been able to destroy that understanding, that quiet boat, that hard kernel, that single hot coal. And since that understanding has not been destroyed, I have not been destroyed. I have not been swallowed up by the symptoms of my mental illness.

But I still have a mental illness. There really is something wrong with my brain. And that's okay.

I have only been rescued from the compulsions, from the worship of the Siren. But I am still in the Wilderness of it. The understanding has not removed this Affliction. One does not get rid of the other. They occupy the same space.

Understanding who Christ is, who you are, and where you're going and what you're supposed to be doing does not make you suffer less, it only changes what Suffering appears to you as: as simple Wilderness rather than god. As symptoms rather than omens.

This Affliction, the thing I call What's Wrong With My Brain lives in me as What Has to Happen. This simple indicative lives in me as an imperative, as an intimidation. But that patient, quiet understanding can turn What Has to Happen back into What's Wrong, can turn a god back into a simple Affliction.

An Affliction Christ bears with me. A Wilderness I walk with Christ.

And this helps you to bear it all quietly. You can have that patient, quiet understanding and still be upset. You can have that patient, quiet understanding and still be miserable. You can have that understanding and still be tempted by despair. You can have that understanding and still be in anguish and distress. This patient, quiet understanding can even be deepened in anguish and distress. It can be deepened in torment and misery. You can have that understanding and still have these Afflictions. You can be made to see and feel horrors, be made to very powerfully feel you are not okay and still understand that you are okay.

Calling this illness What's Wrong may sound like a harsh way of putting it. But calling it that has been a tenderness toward myself. When the Siren is a god, then I'm afraid of it. When it is a Bully, I have to fight it. But when it's What's Wrong, then it's just a vulnerability I take care of. I go from being mad at my brain to wanting to take care of it because it's sick and because it's mine. I go from fighting and hiding it to quietly, patiently leading it. I can offer myself to the brain that I have rather than hate my brain for not being what I wanted.

BECAUSE THIS AFFLICTION CAN OCCUPY the same space as that understanding, I am able both to be profoundly vulnerable and to know that I am profoundly vulnerable, vulnerable to the machinations of my own mind and vulnerable, more importantly, to the anguish of the soul and the Hardness of Heart awakened by this Affliction.

Maybe it can be hard to know what I mean by hardness of heart. The heart, again, is not about what attracts or repels us. It is not about what is thought or felt or haunts or tempts. It is not even, really, about what we long and ache for. It is not even about what pains us or gives us sorrow. The heart is about what is given and what is taken. The heart is about what is offered and what is withheld. The heart is about what is trusted, what is depended on.

As hard as the shame and fear and dread brought on by this Affliction are, by this patient, quiet understanding I know there is something worse than shame and fear and dread it torments me with. This is even something worse than my soul's great anguish over having to live with this illness. Terrible and annihilating forces that they are, there is something worse. In and through that patient, quiet understanding I know that no shame or fear or dread or thought or feeling has disfigured me as profoundly as my dependence on myself, the Hardness of the Heart that is our dependence on ourselves. By the Siren I have only been grieved and wounded terribly. But I have been misshapen by knowing for sure, figuring out, defending myself, and making right. I have only been misshapen by depending on myself. It is by my dependence on myself that I have become disfigured. God and Stranger in my own life.

And the Realm of Ceaseless Cognition has always been the place I've gone to depend on myself, where I go in my head to make sure, figure out, defend myself, and make things right. All those compulsions, bobbing and weaving in a vast, biting, tangled, thrashing nest. Those vast, intoxicating tendrils of thought. Of course, it was only as I was leaving it that I understood it as a Realm, this Haunted House as haunted and as a house, a place I should leave and a place I could leave. For the longest time I simply understood that Realm as who I was. I thought I was that ornate, circuitous, tangled hypervigilance. I thought I was the clinging, dark, shadowy embroidery that fell between me and the world I lived in.

What I know now is that it is a Realm, a Haunted House, the place I am misshapen, my compulsion to depend on myself. And I understand I am too vulnerable to go in there. I am too vulnerable to go into my head, too vulnerable to go in there and figure things out, or make things right, or defend myself, or know for sure. Too vulnerable to go into the Realm of Ceaseless Cognition. Too vulnerable to depend on myself. I will have to depend on Christ instead. There has been nothing in my life more beautiful and harrowing than having to become that patient, quiet understanding.

The Bully, the Accuser, the Siren, What's Wrong, this Affliction has been for me only a kind of terrible Suffering. The only thing it can do is threaten and wound and terrify me. I have only been disfigured by what I'll do to feel okay. I have been most disfigured by what I'll do to not have to feel what the Siren makes me feel: that droning mechanical cry of shame, fear, and dread. I have been most disfigured by what I'll do to not have to see what it makes me see: those horrible intrusive thoughts. I've been most disfigured by where I'll go and what I'll do to avoid the Siren. What I'll do to not feel shame, fear, and dread.

And there is nothing that argues more persuasively, promises more insistently, or demands more savagely to be the clothing of our shame, the casting out of our fear, and the overturning of our dread than our dependence on ourselves. The Realm where I've gone to clothe my own shame, cast out my own fear, overturn my own dread. The Haunted House is where I've hidden from the Siren and made a shrine to myself. It's where I've tried to get away from the symptoms of my illness.

The psychiatric community would say it like this: it's not the obsessions that kill us, it's the compulsions.

In the Christian community, it is called original sin.

The Realm of Ceaseless Cognition is a vast, tangled, tendriled, and tortured landscape with its own terrifying pull.

But that patient, quiet understanding is also a kind of place. It is only that it is a smaller, simpler, sparer, more harrowing, more painful place to be. The Realm is a vast country, and this patient, quiet understanding is only a place to stand, naked, terrified, seemingly alone. What I have in Christ is the simple, painful renunciation of the urges created by my brain, the ability to say no to desires and compulsions that will not just go away. I wish it was more. But that is all it's been: a foothold in the storm of thought and feelings. A Thread in the Wilderness. A boat in the storm. A kernel. A single, hot, burning coal in the wind and rain.

That foothold, that boat, that kernel, is not a place where I do something to be okay. It is a place where I don't. That patient, quiet understanding is the place where I stand with Christ and don't do anything to make things right or win or be okay. It is the place where I don't fix, the place where I don't defend myself, the place where I don't figure things out, and the place where I don't know for sure. The place where it is somehow possible to not engage those compulsions. The place I stand with Christ and endure what it feels like to not do those things. The place where I've learned to stand with Christ by being quiet.

The Realm is the place where I have been disfigured by a dependence on myself, all that constant tangled rumination. But patient, quiet understanding is the place where I am transfigured by my patient, quiet dependence on Christ, by my ability to not think, the place where I stand transfigured with Christ even as I am seemingly disfigured by the Wilderness of what I can be made to think and feel.

It turns out even the horrors I can be made to see and feel can be turned into a time of patient waiting on the Mercy offered in the gospel, with the promise we will not be most changed by the horrors we've been made to see and feel, but by the Mercy we've waited on. And this patient, quiet understanding, though it cannot remove those symptoms, can make every intrusive thought, every grotesque feeling, a time of patient waiting on the Mercy that has been offered. Every horrible thing can become a prayer.

That understanding has been a great gift. It has been a quiet mind to suffer with.

I wish my language could be more precise. More technical. There is no actual realm. My compulsions are not actually a Haunted House. There is no real Wilderness. I am not in a literal boat. I am not a small kernel. You cannot look inside me and find a single, hot, burning coal. A patient, quiet understanding is not really a place. Humility is not actually an inheritance or a foothold. But this is as close as language can get. This is as close as I can get to explaining what having this mental illness feels like, and some kind of way of talking about what it is like to get better.

So, instead of saying that understanding is a foothold, or a place to stand, I will say this understanding has been

My honor in shame.

My courage in fear.

My obedience in dread.

My victory in defeat.

My endurance in Affliction.

My composure in distress.

My shield in accusation.

My deliverance from the hardness of my own heart.

Armed with that patient, quiet understanding—knowing that these warnings and commands are not What Should Happen but only What's Wrong with my brain, and knowing the Realm of Ceaseless Cognition certainly isn't me and isn't even a helpful place to be but is only the place I need to leave and the place I am destroyed—I have been able to do something I count miraculous.

I have been able to stare down the Siren, even as it screams at me. I have been able to leave the Realm of Ceaseless Cognition, even as it pulls on me. Armed with that patient, quiet understanding, I have been able to head somewhere else. Knowing that thoughts and feelings are not gods, I head into the Wilderness of what can be thought and what can be felt. Those thoughts and feelings, this anguish and distress, that scream and pull, are not going anywhere. And yet, I am.

I am passing through them, passing them by. I am headed somewhere else.

And where?

Out of the Realm of Ceaseless Cognition,
Out of my dependence on myself,
Into my dependence on Christ,
Into a future provided by Mercy,
Into the ability to pay attention.

WHERE DOES THAT PATIENT, QUIET trust come from? How do you get into that small boat, find that foothold, become that single, hot coal, that small kernel? How do you become that patient, quiet understanding? Where do you get honor in shame, obedience in dread, courage in fear, endurance in Affliction, composure in distress, and deliverance from the hardness of your own heart? Can a patient, quiet understanding really provide all that? Can humility really offer us this much?

I have titled this section "The Mystery of Our Faith." The mystery of faith is what I mean by patient, quiet understanding: the fear of the Lord, that quiet trust, that quiet reverence, that simple humility.

But what is the mystery of faith?

The mystery of faith is where faith comes from.

I wrote a lot while getting better. I still do. I found that something I wrote, whether a good sentence, a good paragraph, a good turn of phrase, wasn't just a sentence or a paragraph or a turn of phrase. It was a foothold, a place to stand. I wrote a short story when I was recovering from OCD that worked like that. I wrote it without thinking too much, and it taught me about what was happening to me. It was the story of a dead man. The story of Lazarus called out of the tomb, told from his perspective. Here's what I wrote:

My death was still in the room. It was wet and evil and soiled the bandages pulled around me. There was a voice. I woke up because it terrified me. Jesus was a friend but the voice He used to wake me up scared me. It would have sounded angry if it wasn't also glory. It was a voice that made Death and me tremble.

He told me to come out.

I feared the voice more than death. It claimed more than death could, its purposes more inscrutable. It was a voice that held, forevermore, what was next.

And because the voice was not a Stranger's, it terrified me more. It is a thing of terror to call the living God a friend of yours.

I was wrapped so that I hobbled to an opening.

He told other people to unwrap me, which means they had to put their hands on my death so it would be pulled off my hair and eyes.

Perhaps I've lied already. Perhaps this is not the story of how I stared down the Siren and walked out of the Realm of Ceaseless Cognition. Perhaps I am only partly right. Perhaps it is better said this way:

This memoir is the story of how I was freed from the clutches of the Siren and dragged out of the Realm of Ceaseless Cognition by the terrifying fact of Christ and by the recognition of His voice. A terror that is a tenderness, a severity that is also a consolation. I am, of course, trembling, shaking, terrified, but it is my own patient, quiet trust that drags me. I am dragged forward by what I understand, a Mercy that is not felt or even thought but is still, somehow, quietly understood. An understanding of the heart. A Mercy that is only understood because it has been spoken.

It is my own trust that drags me. I have been dragged out into the open, back into life, by my own trust in Christ. I have been led out by what I understand. I am dragged out, kicking and screaming, by my own trust in Christ. And yet it is only within the miraculous power of the Word of God to win that trust, to create the John who understands, the John who trusts Christ.

And what kind of Word is it?

It is the Word of what Christ has done.

It is a strange thing: You can only know Who Christ Is by hearing what Christ has done. That patient, quiet trust, that understanding, that humility, that reverence, the fear of the Lord is the gift and condition and inheritance of those who have heard the gospel and who live hearing what they have already heard. It is only by that Word that I have that patient, quiet understanding. And only by that Word that I become that patient, quiet understanding. It is the only thing that can create and deepen and maintain it. The understanding that Mercy has been offered, that I don't need to do anything to be okay, that something has been done so that I am okay.

This is a world of great shame, fear, and pride and one full of so many Afflictions. And over such things we have no power. All this great shame, fear, dread, and pride is too much to bear and can only be overcome by being spoken to. They are only overcome by hearing what Christ has done. The reason we have not been destroyed is because we have been spoken to.

What, more specifically, is this Word? The Word is Christ has died. Its vindication is Christ is risen. It's fulfillment is Christ will come again.

His hanging there on the cross is, somehow, a Word to us. He has given us His Word. And by that Word, He has given Himself to us.

It is the final Word, but it's a Word I've never gotten over. It has confused me, destroyed me. Exposed and nurtured me. Cut and mended me. It is a Word that I've heard but am not done hearing. A Word of what has been done that is not done with me.

Above all else I know this: it is only by that Word that Christ has given Himself to us. I wish Christ would give Himself some other way, and come to us some other way. But that is how He has done it. Christ will only give Himself to us by the Word of His death.

Is it that simple? Didn't Jesus do anything other than die horribly? Doesn't He appear and work in other ways? Yes, and yet everything He said or did was gathered up and fulfilled in what was said and done there, and everything He is was gathered up and fulfilled in what He is there, and becomes a Word to us, a Word He died to secure, rose to vindicate, ascended to proclaim, and will return to fulfill. His disappearance from us in the flesh was His entrance into the world as this Word, using that Word to pillage and anoint, cast down and build up, through His Spirit and in His fellowship.

The Scriptures tell us that that Word is not just information and not even a story. It is even more than an oath, or even a promise. The hearing of this Word is an event that involves us in the power, promise, and peril of the cross itself. To hear the Word of the cross is to become a part of the Event of the cross. Because it is by that Word that Christ has given Himself to us, to hear it is to become involved in His life. A Word that is His beauty, His company, and His feast so that to hear it is to be seen, to be safe, and to be fed. To hear it is to become someone else.

It is a Word, as I've said, of great promise and peril, of great risk and reward. It is, above all, a Word of Mercy.

It is only by that Word that I can be miserable and upset and still understand that I am okay. That Word is my only place to stand with the symptoms of this illness and understand them as the symptoms of an illness. It is only by that Word that I can have the End of the World as a simple Affliction. The final Word as a simple Wilderness. It is only by that Word that Suffering is not a god that can bully me.

In order to do that, this Word must be nearer to us than the shame, fear, and dread of this Affliction. Christ must be nearer than what I can be made to see and feel. The Word must be as near the thing awakened by the shame, fear, dread of this Affliction: the hardness of heart that is our dependence on ourselves.

The hardness of heart is a blindness we can't even see to get rid of, a dependence on ourselves that we cannot even distinguish from ourselves. And because this pride isn't something we can see to get rid of, and because this hardness of heart isn't something we can even distinguish from ourselves, it is not something we can ever end. We cannot end our own hardness of heart. We cannot end our unwillingness and unbelief. And so in order to bury something so close to us, something we can't even see, something we think we think is the same as ourselves, this Word must be nearer to us than we are to ourselves.

There must be a burial for our hardness of our heart. So that Christ can be for us the things we cannot be for ourselves. Christ must be the burial of our hardness of heart, so that He can be

The clothing of our shame.

The casting out of our fear.

The overturning of accusation.

The enduring of our Affliction.

There is nothing in my life that has been more painful than the overturning of my hardness of heart. There is nothing in the Christian life that will make us come so close to feeling that we are being destroyed. We must be careful when we say the Word is a friend of ours. Until the day of Christ's Return it is a Word that will always stand with us and against us, a Word that stands against our hardness of heart so that it can stand with us in the Wilderness of what can be thought or felt, and be for us all the things we cannot be for ourselves. It is only by that Word that Christ can stand in every place we have stood, and only by that Word that He can be for us the things we cannot be for ourselves.

What sense can we make of this, the near cruelty of this Word of Mercy: Its decision to destroy something very precious to us, something we cling to so closely we think it is us, our very heart and soul, our dependence on ourselves? When Mercy strikes, when Mercy burns, we think we are being destroyed, we think we are being humiliated and crushed, when what is happening is that we are being seen, we are becoming safe, we are being fed, we are being changed by Christ's death and resurrection. We are finally beginning to understand.

How do we begin to contend with the near cruelty of that kind of Mercy? How to articulate that it is Mercy that reveals our need of Mercy and that this is the unbearable charity of the gospel?

In order to proclaim this Word, to trace the way forward that was opened to me by the Mercy that has been spoken, I am going to show you the last three years of my life: a breakdown, a trip to the psych ward, the loss of my career, a slow recovery. And in so doing, the Memory of this Affliction will be asked to come out—that shrieking, ugly, horrible thing. The Past will be told to come out, will be summoned—bully that it is—to become what the Past does not want to become. The Word will be joined to My Affliction the way it has been joined to the bread and wine and the waters of baptism. By that Word, the Memory of this horrible Affliction will be told to come out and become the last thing it wants to be: the proclamation of the gospel rather than the annihilation of myself. The Past will be told to become the Bread of God. A way you and I are fed and nourished by Christ. A way we are seen, a way we are safe, a way we are fed. A way that we finally understand. A way that we are headed somewhere. A way that we become someone else.

In October 2018, the thoughts in my head got so bad I went to a psych ward. It had gotten to the point where I couldn't eat and couldn't move. My heart looked on in terror at the things shown to me by the faulty wiring of my brain. I trembled in grief and fear and sorrow at the horrors I was made to see and feel. My body and mind were not mine. They had become terrifying

Strangers screaming at me in uninterpretable hieroglyphics. My wife drove me in the Subaru while I called my pastor and cried.

The three days I spent in that psych ward were an introduction to deep and unimaginable pain. I had not suffered in that kind of way ever before or since. That experience gave me a body that never felt safe again, a Body That Expected annihilation and dissolution. I came back with a Body That Expected the World to End.

I think of those days often and realize there is little I can do about them, and little I can do with the two years that followed: years when I was consistently taken aback by just how much it was possible to lose, and just how bad it was possible to feel.

Those were bad days, and I cannot make them better. The Past has its own swagger, its own irrevocable privilege, its own unique signature: unlike many other things in life it cannot be repressed or corrected. You can't fix it or get rid of it. The Past has become your body now.

To live with OCD, I've said, is to be vulnerable to the machinations of your own mind, to be incredibly vulnerable to What's Wrong precisely because What's Wrong always presents itself so vividly and actively as What Has to Happen: warnings and commands, screams and pulls, urgencies and urges from bullies and gods. It is an Affliction that lives in me as a powerful, painful intimidation.

But we are not just vulnerable to What's Wrong. We are also vulnerable to the Past, to History, to What Happened to us.

Just as the Siren (this Affliction) lives in me as powerful, painful intimidation, the Past lives in my body as a cringing, crying anticipation. My body expects the world to end and things to fall apart. Just as What's Wrong lives in me as What Should Happen, What Happened lives in my body as What Could Happen. What Happened has not come and gone. It is my body now. It is a Body That Expects the World to End.

What's Wrong and What Happened are both ways that we suffer. History and Affliction, the Siren and the Past, What's Wrong and What Happened, work together in their own special way to destroy us completely. Mind and body, once our home, once our own, break loose and become terrifying Strangers. Mind and body become a terrifying Wilderness we make our way through, a Wilderness where we wonder if we will be destroyed by what we can be made to see and feel.

But Suffering, whether by History or Affliction, is not primarily about what we have been made to see and feel or what has been done. Suffering is primarily about what has been taken, and what can be taken: honor, health, safety, will, control. Our minds and bodies, even as we still have them, feel taken from us. A Wilderness is not only a place where anything can happen, where the worst can be seen and the worst can be felt; it is also the place where everything can be taken.

And this makes remembering a problem. If I can't avoid What's Wrong, surely in some way I can block out What Happened. If I can't avoid this illness, I should definitely avoid remembering, right? If What Happened is a horror, if it is the unmentionable, and if it lives in me as the cringing, crying anticipation of What Could Happen, then why would I want to remember? Why go back to an old humiliation and be humiliated? Why go back to an old violation and be violated? Why go back to what was lost and lose again? Why go back to what was lost and have more taken? Why go back to What Happened then and risk losing what I have now? Why go back to What Happened and be devoured?

What Happened is a dangerous place and remembering an adventure undertaken with great peril. To remember is often to be further disfigured by What Happened, especially if what happened was the traumatic and unmentionable.

When What Happened is traumatic or unmentionable, then Memory turns on you and becomes something else. It is no longer a companion, trying to help you remember who you were. Memory is now a predator, lurking around every corner, trying to destroy who you are. As those who have lost loved ones can attest, when something bad happens even memories that once consoled and held you together can suddenly transform into wild things coming after you. Memory, once such a gentle companion, can become a very real and surprising threat to self. Mind, body, and Memory become terrifying Strangers.

We don't get to remember and stay the same. Memory is too awful and powerful. And so the question is, Will I be transformed or destroyed by remembering? Will I be transfigured or further disfigured by what I remember?

I can only speak for myself. I can only talk about what I've found: that if I walk back into the Past with a dependence on myself, I will not make it out. If I walk back into What Happened—into the Wilderness of what has been done and what I can be made to see and feel—with the intention of clothing my shame, casting out my own fear, defying my own dread, bearing my own History, overturning every accusation and enduring my own Affliction, I will be destroyed. If I go back into History trying to fix or defend or make it right, I will only be misshapen by what I remember. Remembering will only make me a disfigured god and Strangers in my own life. Remembering will only cast me into exile.

If we can walk back into the awful and the unmentionable with a dependence on Christ, perhaps we can be transfigured. I don't know if we will feel better or worse, but my hope is that even if what is remembered is awful, even if it wounds us terribly, we will still be more like ourselves for remembering. We will somehow be more like servants and guests in His life rather than gods and Strangers in ours.

I use the word "perhaps" because, though I have found a way back into What Happened that has been, ultimately, painfully, life-giving, I don't know whether you will and whether you should.

And I mean this seriously. No one should walk back into the Past naively. The Past, in conjunction with such annihilating forces as shame, fear, Affliction, and our dependence on ourselves, has a very real power to cross out, swallow up, snuff out.

I have only been able to go back into What Happened, and with it the active threat of annihilation and being swallowed up, because such things as Scripture, prayer, friends, therapy, time, and writing have secured for me a surefootedness and generosity with What Happened that was not available to me when it was my shrieking and vivid present tense. I've only been able to go into the Past with the understanding that Mercy has been offered. I have only been able to go back into What Happened with the patient, quiet understanding of who Christ is and who I am, where I'm going and what I'm supposed to be doing.

Memory offers such a profound threat to the self that the only safe way back into What Happened is with understanding won for me by hearing what someone else has done. I can only go back into the unmentionable with a patient, quiet understanding that has been

My honor in shame,
My courage in fear,
My obedience in dread,
My endurance in Affliction,
My withstanding of History,
My composure in distress,
My shield in accusation,
My deliverance from the hardness of my own heart.

And we only have that understanding when we know by that Word that Christ has pledged Himself to us, when we know by that Word that Christ is all of the things we cannot be ourselves. When we understand He is

The clothing of our shame.

The casting out of our fear.

The overturning of accusation.

The bearing of History.

The enduring of Affliction.

The burial of the Hardness of the Heart.

I mean it. Memory needs a shepherd. Otherwise it has tremendous power to deform. It has been my experience that only Christ knows what to do with Memory, how to shepherd and consecrate it by His Word. Only He can make it transfigure us. We cannot make these things holy. Christ knows this. Only He can make these horrible things a way that we are seen and safe and fed and become ourselves again. Memory is too powerful and too painful to be made holy by anything else. Christ who has drawn near by His Word.

But is this even true? Am I lying? Can something lived as tragedy be remembered as deliverance? Can the things that disfigured then transfigure now? How is it that something that was terrible when lived is beautiful when written? Something that, in the present tense, was ashes in my mouth is, in Memory, a way I feed on Christ and find myself ready to storm the gates of hell? Is it really true that to remember well, to remember by faith, is to be transfigured by Christ even if what is remembered is horrible?

Can remembering something horrible really turn us into something that is not horrible?

And yet, does it matter whether we want to remember? The Past cannot be repressed or corrected. It has become our bodies now. Like a storm destroying the house. The storm is not gone. It is the house that has been destroyed. There is no option but remembering. We suffer either way.

"SUFFERING IS A MYSTERY BY which we are driven either to humility or despair."

I wrote this once in the corner of a journal, and it has been a comfort and a challenge and an accusation ever since. The two kinds of Suffering mentioned above—What's Wrong and What Happened—have been too powerful for me to stay the same. History and Affliction have become our minds and bodies. We must give Suffering its due: it's not going anywhere, it cannot be ignored, and it will not leave us the same. The Suffering is our own minds and bodies. Minds and bodies that, even as we live with them, are no longer ours. They have become terrifying Strangers.

We cannot answer Suffering, and especially not our own Suffering. Suffering that has left us too confused and wounded. It is too close to us.

And yet Suffering demands an answer.

Otherwise our Suffering will become an intolerable bully, joining hands with such terrible things as fear, shame, dread, and the Hardness of the Heart. An answer to Suffering must be made. Otherwise the world will be rendered meaningless and intolerable. Otherwise, History and Affliction will reveal this world to be a total loss.

I have to think of Christ's own relationship to History and Affliction. That the worst thing that could happen to a person happened to Christ. The worst things a person could be made to see and feel were seen and felt by Christ. Everything that could be taken from a person was taken from Christ.

And the worst that could happen, and the worst that could be seen and felt, and everything that could be taken, all came to a point in the nails driven into His hands and is now a Word mentioned forever in His own body. And now all that Suffering means something else. Every good and bad thing has been changed, not by having got better or worse, but by Christ's proximity to it. History and Affliction have become His body, and made holy by His body.

Jesus kept the scars and decided to stay in heaven as the Christ who died. And when He did that He took the crucifixion, and with it all of human pain, everything that could be seen and felt and done and taken, into the throne room of God. What's Wrong and What Happened were allowed in the throne room of God. They were, in fact, ushered in with singing. History and Affliction, in this way, were overcome but not removed. Neither repressed nor corrected. History and Affliction were, rather, consecrated. They were still somehow there. Held there by the scars kept in heaven, but they were made something else. They were made holy. Again, not because they had got better or worse, but because they had now been mentioned forever in Christ's own body. Those horrors are made holy because of the body that made them holy. He bore them and bears them in His body. A body broken for us and blood shed for us. A broken body and spilled blood that is the Word for us. The only thing that can make anything holy.

By that Word, the surprising pain of being human—and with it all things horrible and excruciating and unmentionable—is no longer, strictly speaking, ours. What's Wrong and What Happened have been offered to the Father through Christ's body. Everything that can be seen and felt is already a psalm. And has been made a psalm through Christ's body. Everything that can be taken from us is already prayer, and has been made a prayer through Christ's body. Suffering is not a dead end; it has become a movement toward God through Christ's body. And can be trusted through His broken body. And now everything we can be made to see or feel, everything that can be done or taken, must lead us to Christ through His broken body.

Christ has taken full responsibility for the surprising pain of being human. Everything that can be seen, felt, done, or taken has been given back to us as this Word. And only Christ has done this.

History and Affliction, this kind of terrible Suffering, is a mystery answered only by Christ. By Christ's Sufferings and not by me. He is the only one who has taken responsibility for human Suffering and has taken responsibility for it in His very flesh. It is only His to answer. And this is the answer He has made.

He will answer it only by His proximity to it, only by having all of it driven into His hands and given back to us as Himself. The answer to Suffering can only ever be Christ's answer. It can never be ours.

Many people who have had terrible things happen are not better for it, and probably not better for remembering it. We wound each other needlessly by charging into the Past and claiming a naive victory over terrible Suffering. History and Affliction do not have any intention of being my friend. It has become clear to me over the years that what the Past and my OCD want to do is embarrass and threaten and kill me. They are not kind, they are not friends. It is not within the overt power of trauma, crashes, AIDs, or dementia, or within OCD itself, to be a friend to me, but only within the subversive power of the gospel to do so, to make them an unwilling friend of my life in Christ. And that is not something that can ever happen by effort or sorrow. It is only by that Word, the Word of His death, that our Pasts, our illnesses, are allowed to threaten and thrash and demolish everything except what they have been condemned to deepen: the patient, quiet understanding of who Christ is, and who I am. This will only happen gradually, and eventually. The endurance of Suffering is a mystery taken into Christ's own torn flesh and delivered to us through the event of hearing His Word. The gift of humility, and the enduring of Suffering, is the creation of His Word, a Word that involves us in the power, promise, and peril of His victory. The vigilant hearing of the gospel is the patient endurance of History and Affliction. Christ has taken responsibility for our endurance, and He has done so through the hearing of His Word.

And now, no matter how vivid, how shrieking they appear, What's Wrong and What Happened have a yoke to bear, having now been trapped in Christ's body. History and Affliction must release us from the verdict they have spoken over us and begin to serve our life in Christ, our life with the One who captured and consecrated them in His flesh. Even our loss reveals Christ to us. All loss has been taken into His flesh. Now even the Past must give us Christ and give us back to ourselves. Now even what is lost must deepen our understanding of who Christ is and who we are, where we're going and what we're supposed to be doing. By that Word, History and Affliction must render to us a simple life of faith, hope, and love.

But this has been my answer. I cannot make it yours. At the heart of my own Suffering, I have only found someone who can be depended on. It is only by that Word that He has given Himself to me as someone to be depended on, and only by that Word that I understand that I will not be most changed by What's Wrong or What Happened but by what I depend on.

I will be most changed by what I worship. To worship is to be changed by what you depend on.

The only way I have ever been, or could ever be, transfigured by thoughts this disturbing, feelings this grotesque, and a Past this annihilating is if they are something I trust Christ with. I have learned that even if I cannot get rid of them that by patient endurance, I can still trust Christ with what they mean. So that even these horrors can be turned into a time of patient waiting on the Mercy offered in the gospel. And Christ's promise is that we will not be most changed by the horrors in the Wilderness but by the Mercy we have waited on.

When we know that Suffering cannot deprive us of Christ because all Suffering has been taken into His very body, a body He freely hands over to us as His Word, I believe something incredible can happen over time: Suffering will no longer be able to wield the power of shame, because we are not ashamed of it. Suffering will no longer be able to wield the power of fear, because we are not afraid of it. It will no longer be able to awaken the hardness of our heart or the despair in our soul, because now that Christ has given Himself to us by Suffering, we can trust him with what Suffering has taken. And Suffering can just be Suffering, something Christ bears with us, for us in His own body. A body He now gives freely every time we hear the Word and take the bread and wine. We will be able to live with What's Wrong and What Happened as the Wilderness He endures with us. So that we will not be bullied by Suffering, and will have the power to face it quietly, with the understanding that Mercy has been offered.

AGAIN, I WANT TO BE careful. Suffering, by itself, does not have any meaning. It only ruins, it only takes away. It is only given meaning by Christ's proximity to it. And He only gives meaning to it by enduring, bearing, and overcoming it.

By that Word, Christ does not explain away History and Affliction, but becomes the enduring of History and bearing of Affliction. He has given His Word that He will be this for us. And He can only be this for us because He took responsibility for it. Whose torn flesh is the enduring and the bearing and the taking of responsibility.

But He can only be the bearing of History and the enduring of Affliction if He is also the burial of our Hardness of the Heart. It is a Word that must be the burial of our Hardness of the Heart so it can stand with us in the enduring and bearing of History and Affliction. A History and Affliction that will be a Wilderness that will either drive us to humility or despair, that has simply done too much and taken too much for us to ever be the same or return to anything that could be called normal.

The difference between humility and despair is often so hidden as to be unobservable. If you do not believe me, read Job, Ecclesiastes, or the Psalms. There is only one real distinction between humility and despair, and the distinction is only made by the Word of what Christ has done. It is only now that Christ has given Himself to us by Suffering that we can trust Him with what Suffering has taken from us: our honor, strength, safety, security, our own sense of self. Our minds, bodies, and memories that have become terrifying Strangers.

It turns out, in this Wilderness, anything we trust Christ with—anything we give to him—will transform us, that is, turn us into simple servants and guests of the Mercy offered in His gospel. Anything we trust Him with will turn us into who we are, into people who are headed somewhere, headed toward the future provided by Mercy. And anything we don't trust him with—anything we keep from him—will destroy us, turn us into who we aren't, into misshapen gods and Strangers. People who are headed nowhere.

Because He kept the scars, because He can be trusted with what has been taken from us, because what is seen and felt and done and taken is now His body, we know the Past and this Affliction, without ceasing to be the horrible thing that it is, is not the final Word or the End of the World and does not get to tell us everything about ourselves.

It is important to make this point. There are things so secret and painful and awful that only Christ can make them holy. He is the only one who can, and He will only do it in His time and with His own gentleness and severity. Only Christ can make hard things holy things. The horrible and the unmentionable will only be made holy by Christ's proximity to the horrible and the unmentionable. A mystery taken in His body that does not give us an answer but only the mystery of faith. A faith born through hearing, led in prayer, established by offering.

AGAIN, DO I MEAN THIS? And how could I possibly mean this? How have I experienced this?

Because History and Affliction have taken so much from me, because they live in me now as the terrifying Stranger of mind and body, what History and Affliction have revealed is that I am vulnerable.

Mind and body are terrifying and elusive Strangers that will not leave, that I cannot fix or manage, cannot make better or make go away. The very fact that History and Affliction have become this to me, have become my terrorized body and my stubborn, creaming mind, make them something I always want to control, manage, and fix.

Who wants a Siren and a Body That Expects the World to End?

But the very things History and Affliction awaken—my dependence on myself, my desire to fix, control, and manage, my desire to figure out, know for sure, defend myself, and make things right—are the very things that History and Affliction ridicule and destroy and expose as never ever, ever, ever enough. The thing they awaken, our dependence on ourselves, is the very thing they take away.

We are gods trying to control What's Wrong and What Happened, and then, when we cannot, we are Strangers, exiles, cast out by What's Wrong and What Happened. When we cannot fix or console our body and mind, they cast us out.

History and Affliction show us what cannot be made right, what we cannot be for ourselves, that we cannot clothe our own shame, cast out our own fear, endure our own Affliction. It is History and Affliction that show us what Christ will have to be for us if we are going to be okay. If we are going to have a future.

And that is how remembering has been helpful: to go back into What Happened as a Christian, to go back to that place where life was not something that could be fixed or managed, where Life as I Would Have It had come to an end, to go back to something I cannot make right. To have arrived back at that place is to have arrived among the sacred.

Perhaps for someone else it is no great help to locate that vulnerability, that helplessness. There is maybe nothing for him or her in remembering but more helplessness. And that helplessness may not be sacred for them. It may be an annihilation.

But it has not been for me.

For me, to go back into the What Happened is to understand myself as wounded, limited, selfish, vulnerable. And to understand myself as vulnerable, wounded, limited, selfish is to understand that Mercy has been offered. To have found that place of complete dependence is to have found my dependence on Christ. And to have found my dependence on Christ is to have found the person of Christ. And to have found the person of Christ is to have found a Mercy nearer than what can be seen or felt, more than what can be done or taken.

In the Wilderness of what we can be made to see and feel, of what can be done or taken, we learn what Christ will have to be for us if things are going to be okay, that He will have to be more for us than we ever thought He could or should. And by realizing what we cannot be for ourselves, and what Christ will have to be, we are given a stunning, solemn, reverent fear of who Christ is. A humility that is our way forward, an understanding of the heart that is our place to stand. And we will be led through the Wilderness as that patient, quiet understanding, led into the future by what we understand.

By the subversive power of the gospel, History and Affliction have not been the sucking, annihilating vortex they have intended, but have become, instead, the Wilderness where I have been freed from my dependence on myself. History and Affliction have only deepened my understanding of who Christ is, and who I am, and where I'm going. They have been a terrible Wilderness where I have become neither god nor Stranger but servant and guest of the Mercy offered in His gospel.

If this is true, then how to begin to talk about such things? How do I speak well about a mental breakdown and a hospitalization that was personally catastrophic and also, somehow, the Word of God to me? A way that Christ gave Himself to me, and gave me to Himself? How can I begin to talk about what it is like to be acted on, painfully and gradually, by the hearing of that

Word? The hearing of that Word in this Wilderness? A Word that bears its fruit in the profanity of the human heart only patiently and painfully over time?

THERE IS A PROBLEM WITH History and Affliction.

The trouble with Affliction is that there is no such thing as just an Affliction. There is also the one who was afflicted.

The trouble with what happened is there's no such thing as just What Happened. There's also the one it happened to.

We trust Christ not just with what was taken, but with the one it was taken from.

There is no harder relationship than our relationship to the one who was afflicted, and the one the worst happened to, the one everything was taken from. There is no more difficult or painful or mysterious thing than our relationship to ourselves. The most difficult and painful and mysterious thing I've had to do is trust Christ with the one who was afflicted, the one who was abandoned, the one everything was taken from, the one the worst has already happened to, the one who was made to see and feel horrors. There is nothing more difficult, painful, and mysterious than to trust Christ with that person, to trust Christ with our relationship to ourselves.

To remember What Happened is to turn our face to the one it happened to, and to be with that person. And no one wants to do that. It is too painful. We are all sorry that it happened, and we don't want to deal with the one it happened to. Even if it is ourselves.

I have had to meet myself. I have had to meet the one who was afflicted, the one the Past happened to, the one everything was taken from.

I've had to meet him and he is screaming.

He is screaming because he is Suffering. Even still. He is screaming because he is in misery and torment and great distress. He is screaming because of his unbearable dissatisfaction.

It took time to write this book, and to write it to the one who was afflicted, and the one it happened to. To learn how to approach him. It took time to find the John who stalked the halls of the psych ward three years ago, to find him back in the hospital muttering to himself with a shattered brain, and to not hate him. To not hate him in his misery, to not hate him in his torment, to not hate him in his great distress. It is hard not to try to restore my dignity now by hating him then.

This is a strange thing, and something I've never understood but that has been my own experience: that we depend on ourselves by hating ourselves. It is my suspicion that what we are trying to do by hating ourselves is to clothe our shame and make things right. There is no burden heavier than trying to make things right by hating ourselves. By hating ourselves, we try to make ourselves gods by making ourselves Strangers, and so we are torn in two. It is an addiction we cannot quit, a blindness we cannot see, a compulsion we cannot distinguish from ourselves.

And it is something only a dependence on Christ can gradually heal us of.

I do not hate him anymore. But there was, and is, a cringing embarrassment at finding him again in Memory and presenting him before us in these pages.

I've learned to call the John I've found in Memory the Howling Boy. He isn't What's Wrong or What Happened; he is the one who suffered this Affliction, the one who bore the brunt of History. He isn't the mind's intimidation, the body's anticipation. He is the soul's anguish. My unbearable dissatisfaction. He is the one made to suffer the mind's painful, powerful intimidation, made to suffer the body's cringing, crying anticipation. Made to suffer the terrible misery and burden of it. The Howling Boy is my word for the anguish of the soul. He is the wounded, selfish, alienated person that I was, that I am, and that I will be until Christ comes back.

It has taken me years of wading and walking through the Wilderness of symptoms to finally find him where he always was, in that psych ward. He has been hard to find. It is hard to distinguish between the Howling Boy and the Siren, between the Howling Boy and the trauma. It is hard to distinguish between what he is really feeling and what he has been made to feel by the terrifying Strangers of mind and body. It is hard to distinguish between the greater, deeper, heaving, wrenching shame, fear, dread of a soul in anguish and the droning, mechanical fear, shame, dread of mental anguish or the cringing anticipation of a body in constant anticipation and threat. I cannot always tell if I'm being bullied by the Siren, throttled by trauma, or if the Howling Boy is trying to tell me something.

I have made my way through the mind's powerful intimidation, through the body's cringing anticipation. And found my soul's anguish. And have called him the Howling Boy.

There he is, still Suffering after all these years.

Can you see him?

There he is now, a tall, shaggy-haired man in his late twenties, walking up and down the hallway of the psych ward with a small gown and no shoes. He has two master's degrees, he preaches at his small church.

But there he is. In the psych ward. Howling quietly to himself.

And the question is, Why is he a boy, and why is he howling?

It took a long time, but I think I know now.

He is howling because his world is not safe. And this is his great fear.

He is howling because the world does not want him. And this is his great shame.

He is howling because his body and mind have become what he does not understand and the cause of great Suffering. They have become a great gaping maw threatening to swallow him whole. He is in the fierce grip of forces beyond his control.

And he is a boy because, like all children, he has not yet got over the fact that the world is not as he would have it. He hasn't got over what has been taken, and what could be taken so suddenly: his body and his mind. The sudden taking of body and mind now lives in him as an unprecedented and unbearable dissatisfaction. The mind's intimidation and the body's anticipation have caused in his soul a great shame, fear, and grief, and despair. I am still so surprised to find this part of me, the part of me that could be so vulnerable, so wounded, so lonely, so selfish, and so upset. Not the screaming of the mind, not the throttling of the body, but the soul's great anguish, felt so powerfully he cannot stand it. A soul that cries out that life is intolerable and it is alone.

Why is he even in the psych ward? The aggravated symptoms of his OCD have been misunderstood as potential psychosis. He was locked in an empty cell under the assumption that he may be a threat to himself or others, and will continue to be locked in a facility for the next three days. And this has traumatized him, made him feel he is about to be snuffed out, crossed out, tossed out, written off, completely annihilated. And every way he has ever known to depend on himself and get himself out of something like this has only made everything worse. History and Affliction—and the Strangers they have made of body, mind, and soul—have now shown him so stunningly that life is not something that can be fixed or managed or controlled, something that can be made right, have all but convinced him that life is intolerable and he is alone. He walks the hallways in the agony of what he can be made to see and feel and under the almost complete and screaming certainty that his life is intolerable and he is alone.

And because he has suffered so much, and because so much has been taken, and because this Affliction is bearing down on him with such bewildering intensity because he is sure he is about to die, he is going to make a tragic decision about What He'll Do to Be Okay. He will make a decision with the Hardness of the Heart. He is going to try to defend himself, figure things out, make things right, and know for sure, and this will only make everything much worse.

The reason we don't want to remember What Happened is simple: we can't stand or possibly deal with the person it happened to. Their distress that can so easily become our distress, their intolerable Suffering that will so easily become ours. The one thing we can't stand about those prior versions of ourselves is the way they can make us feel again. The Howling Boy is all the things I don't want to feel. And I have come here to be with him. He is my exile. An intolerable, unacceptable, inconsolable prior version of myself. And I have come here to be with him.

I have to go back into What Happened, to go back there with the time machine that is my own traumatized body, to go back there with a Body That Expects the World to End. I have to go out there to where he was crushed, where he was completely vulnerable and exposed. And to stand there with him. Not to fix him, or change him, but to stand with him as he waits to get annihilated. And to wait to be annihilated with him.

Being with him threatens what I have valued most since, which is the feeling of stability. The cozy feeling that all is well that I have managed to cultivate for myself by better eating, good therapy, diligent exercise, and strict routine. My search for him has been the hunt for something more important than stability, which is reconciliation.

I've decided to remember What Happened so I can turn my face to the one it happened to. And to tell him, by standing with him, that I am not ashamed of him, that I am not afraid of him, and that he is welcome in my life. His grief, his anger, his agony, his great sadness are welcome in my life.

Memory come back to me.

Memory come back to me.

Memory come back to me.

Howling boy, come back to me.

Howling boy, come back to me.

Howling boy, come back to me.

I have to go out to where he was destroyed, and listen to him, and stand there with him. Standing with him is standing with the hardest parts of myself. And I can only stand there with him by that Word. With the Word that is our reconciliation.

To remember like this, to meet him like this, is to feel everything again, all of his anguish and distress, and to feel like I will be destroyed by what I'm feeling. And gazing at him, I am undone. I've decided not to ignore him, not to turn my face from him. But I also can't help him. And that's when he looks at me and lunges for me for, to fix it, to make it okay. But I can't fix it, or make it okay. And that's what he's screaming for. He's screaming for what he wants me to be for him. That's what he's screaming I have to be for him.

And there is perhaps nothing more painful than what I can't be for him, nothing more painful than what I can't be for myself.

I can't clothe his shame.

I can't rescue him in his distress.

I can't get rid of all his fear.

I can't explain to him why he's Suffering so much.

I can't make it right.

I am not the Mercy that has been offered. I can only understand that Mercy has been offered. I can only approach the Howling Boy with that understanding. I can only approach my soul's anguish as that patient, quiet understanding. I can only stand with his unbearable dissatisfaction. And by standing there bear witness that it is not unbearable.

It has taken a long time for me to be quiet enough to meet with him. Suffering makes us afraid of Suffering. What Happened makes us afraid of the one it happened to. The deeper my understanding of who Christ is, the quieter I have become, the more able I am to face him, to stand with him, the longer I've been able to stand there, to offer him hospitality, to make myself available to what he is trying to tell me. To be a better kind of company.

I can only be with him by writing this sentence. I can only be present with him in his Affliction.

Of course the Siren hates him, and tells me everything about him is intolerable, unacceptable, and deeply wrong. And of course, my body, my trauma, tells me he is a threat to me. That everything he feels, everything he is, makes him a threat to me. That he is ruined and that he will only ruin me. My body waits for him to ruin me. But I have come all the way out here to be with him, to meet with him, to pay attention to him.

I can only stand there with the Howling Boy, with the hardest parts of myself, and behold, and be patient, and bear witness.

To what?

To what?

To what?

To the Mercy offered in the gospel. I am here to offer the gospel to a prior version of myself.

I do not want to look at the Howling Boy if I can't fix him. If I can't make it better, then I can't deal with him. If I can't be god for him, then he must be a Stranger to me. But I cannot forget him, cannot abandon him, cannot hide him, because he is the John to whom Mercy was offered. It is that John—and not the John who is working hard and doing well and who is stable and not crazy—to whom the Lord has offered His Mercy. This John with his intrusive thoughts, this John who is terrified of what he might be made to think or feel. This John whose grip on reality has become undone by the faulty wiring of his brain. Whose grip on this world and himself has been undone by What's Wrong with his brain. This John who is sure his life is over. Who is helpless, hopeless, full of such anger, sorrow, tension, and uncertainty. Overwhelmed with such sudden and staggering loss to his livelihood and sanity. Overwhelmed with what can be taken and how it can be taken. How fast your body and mind can be taken completely or crush you completely. Surprised by what he feels and how powerfully it is felt. Battered around by how bad it is possible to feel, by what he can be made to feel. Meeting him, knowing him, turning my face toward him will either leave me better or worse. Transfigured, disfigured. It will not leave me the same. He is too powerful, his anguish has too much to say, and what he has to say is too painful to hear for me to be the same.

How do you say that What Happened to you isn't welcome in your life, or that the Memory of What Happened can only deform you? It is like saying the person it happened to isn't welcome in your life. But that is the person who has been addressed by Christ. Who has been seen by Christ. Who has been asked to behold His beauty, who has asked to be patient with His company, who has been invited to His feast.

And so I am here to offer the gospel to an intolerable version of myself. The one who is howling because life is intolerable and he is alone. To declare peace between us. So that we are not gods and Strangers to one another.

I am here, and I am here to tell him he has been forgiven.

Why would someone who suffered terribly need to be forgiven?

Because the forgiveness of sins is not for people who have done something wrong. It is for people who are bound.

Because that is our only way out. The only way out is to be forgiven.

Why?

Because only in the forgiveness of sin is there a tenderness and severity that can separate shame, fear, and humiliation from the way we've controlled it. Because the forgiveness of sin is the only thing that can possibly untangle our own pain from the hidden and idolatrous ways we've managed it. Our soul's anguish from our heart's pride: a distinction that simply isn't available to us. Because it is only the forgiveness of sin that can stand against the Hardness of the Heart and stand with us in our distress, that can heal wounds and bury our hardness of heart, that knows what needs to be mended and what needs to be driven out and overturned. The forgiveness of sin is the only way it can be done without cruelty. It is only the forgiveness of sin that can meet us in our place of deepest need and our place of deepest bondage. And we don't even know it. Because our pride runs deeper than anything we could ever call pride. Because we are helpless in our rebellion, unable to do anything but disbelieve.

Because we wounded, selfish people are such a mixture of pain and promise, of prophetic witness and self-deception, that we are uninterpretable to others and a deep mystery to ourselves.

WE THINK THE FORGIVENESS OF sin is the avoiding of punishment or the evasion of responsibility. We think it means we're not in trouble anymore. We think it means we did something wrong.

But that isn't what it means. The forgiveness of sin means we cannot end our own unbelief or own unwillingness. It means we cannot end the Hardness of the Heart, our own opposition to God.

And we forget how sin is forgiven.

We forget the forgiveness of sin is not an excuse; it is a revelation and an offering. It is the revelation of who Christ is by the gracious offer of Himself. When Christ gave Himself to us as the forgiveness of sin, He revealed what He was like. And Christ buries our hardness of heart and makes provision for the soul's anguish by revealing who He is and what He's like.

Now that Christ has died, He has become this Word of forgiveness. With the forgiveness of sin He has plundered the territory of Satan. A Word that was first preached in hell when He descended to the dead, then preached in the Land of Sin and Death in the Wilderness of Exile to the scattered disciples, finally preached in our churches around the table, the blood and the wine.

The Howling Boy walks the psych ward but also sits cowering and bound in his own Haunted House. Like the first disciples when Jesus had risen from the dead and they hadn't even realized it yet.

I'm there with him. I've come here to be with him.

And Christ appears in the room. We don't know how He got there, we don't know how He found us.

The Howling Boy starts screaming. All is lost. Everything is wrong. The Worst Has Happened. Everything has been taken. It is too much. It is too much.

And Christ shows us the scars.

And we know.

All is lost. Everything was taken. The Worst Has Happened. But it is too late. The Word has been spoken. Christ has given Himself to us. A Word mentioned forever in His own body.

The Worst Has Happened. Everything is wrong. But it is too late. Christ has given Himself to us. And now that Christ has given Himself to us, we have been given back to God, to ourselves, and to each other.

Now that Christ has given Himself to us, there is no shame; it has been clothed. There is no fear; it has been cast out. There is no accusation; it has been overturned. There are no wounds; they have been mended. There is no Hardness of the Heart; it has been buried forever. And Christ has provided for the soul's unbearable dissatisfaction.

This is the Word that has been spoken. And hearing It is the burying of the Hardness of the Heart, the clothing of the shame, the casting out of the fear, the overturning of the lies, and the providing for the soul.

I have come to the Howling Boy bearing this Word of forgiveness. For trying to fix him, get rid of him. Telling him what I know now, that the answer to his Suffering is something only Mercy knows. It is only something Christ can tell him, and something we will both have to wait to hear. I have come to offer him Christ, and to offer Christ as our reconciliation. As the end of our hostility. To the damage he's done to me, to the damage I've done to him. To my hatred of him, my hatred of myself.

Christ is revealed as the forgiveness of sin. And we are revealed as sinners in need of forgiveness. The Howling Boy is not crazy or ruined but a sinner in need of forgiveness. I am not stable or capable but a sinner in need of forgiveness. Our sin is an occasion for Christ's revelation of Himself. Our Hardness of the Heart is not defeated by coercion but by revelation. And because He is the forgiveness of sin,

To be forgiven is to be seen, to be safe, to be fed.

To be forgiven is to be changed, and to finally understand.

To be forgiven is to be headed somewhere.

In God's economy, sinners are honored guests, faithful servants of the Mercy offered in the gospel.

I have come to tell him he is an honored guest. I have come to tell him I am not afraid of him, I am not ashamed of him, and to tell him he is welcome in my life. That I cannot provide him a future but that a future has been provided. I want to tell him he is welcome to the future provided by Mercy. He is headed toward joy.

Why remember What Happened?

What Happened is the pit from which Christ rescues the one it happened to.

WE PROCLAIM THE MYSTERY OF OUR FAITH

The Word, the Way, and the Amen

PART II

WAY AND INTENTION

"THE WORD HAS BEEN SPOKEN. The only thing left is to say amen."

I woke up one morning with these words on my heart. It was like my heart was a stubborn block of wood and this understanding had been carved into it. At the time, I was in recovery and facing a ministry of increasing hardship and complexity. I had a ministry with people on the street, and people on the street reminded me of myself: mentally ill, though more so. Anxious, irritable, though more so. Traumatized, though more so. Barely holding on, but more so.

I would wake up with a Body That Expected the World to End, a contracted chest and strangled throat, simply not knowing What Could Happen to them, what I should do with them or for them. I woke up in a world where anything could be done to me and them and everything could be taken from me and them. I woke up facing their terrifying vulnerability and mine. I woke up in a Wilderness that does not honor what's supposed to happen or let us know what's going to happen.

In that Wilderness, in my bed, and with that terrifying vulnerability, the Lord carved that understanding into my heart.

"The Word has been spoken. The only thing left is to say amen."

There is nothing in this life more beautiful and harrowing than the understanding of who Christ is.

In the Wilderness we learn that Christ is not only the Word we have been given, He is the Amen we've been promised.

He is the Amen to the Word He has already spoken. I understood I was not the Word that had been spoken but that I and all these awful, beautiful, fragile people had been included somehow, beautifully, mysteriously, painfully, harrowingly, in the Amen.

I understood, just as the Word had been pledged, that an Amen had been promised.

In the Wilderness, we are gathered and dragged by the Word toward the Amen. And we are dragged through His Spirit. The same Christ who left the perfect Amen of heaven made His way through the Wilderness of History and Affliction to become that Word for us in our place of deepest need and bondage. That Word of forgiveness. The Word that Christ has died, a Word of Mercy, a Word for the heart's understanding and the soul's anguish. By that Word, Christ has clothed our shame, cast out our fear, endured our Afflictions, overturned all verdicts, and buried the Hardness of the Heart forever. And by that Word Christ has given Himself to us. The gospel, above all things, is about what has been given.

We have been given Christ's death. And by His death Christ has given Himself to us.

The Christ who made His way into the Wilderness to become that Word for us now leads us through the Wilderness through His Spirit. Through His Spirit we are led from the Word He has spoken to the Amen He has promised. This tension between the Word we are led from and the Amen we are led to is the tension of trying to live. Through the Spirit, the Word that was spoken now leads us in the Wilderness as the struggle to say amen. Through His Spirit, the Christ who offered Mercy now leads us in the Wilderness as our cry for Mercy. Through His Spirit, the Christ who said "It is finished" now leads us in the Wilderness with groans too deep for words.

What we are going to need in a world where anything can be seen, felt, done, or taken and can turn body, mind, and soul into screaming Strangers is a way to return to His Word and be led to that amen. We learn we cannot do this ourselves; we learn Christ is not only the Word and the Amen. Christ is not just What's Been Given and What's Been Promised. He is also the Way, our return to What's Been Given and our heading toward What's Been Promised. This is what I believe a life in His Spirit is. A life in His Spirit means Christ is not only the Word and the Amen but also the Way. In the Wilderness we learn Christ is the Word, the Way, and the Amen. Christ is the rescue, the leading, the fulfillment of the trust we have in Him.

I HAVE LEARNED TO PUT IT to myself simply. This is the map I've made, the way I've learned to talk to myself about it:

The crucified Christ is the Word we've been given, the forgiveness of sin, the revelation of who God is and what God is like. Christ revealed who God is by giving Himself to us, so that the crucified Christ is the glory of God. We are rescued by that revelation. The Word reveals who Christ is, and we are changed by who Christ is, and changed into who we are. His Word is the Mercy we behold by hearing.

We are led in the Wilderness by the crucified and risen Christ. The crucified and risen Christ is the Way, returning us to What's Been Given, and leading us to What's Been Promised. He does this by His Spirit. His Spirit is the Mercy we are patient with through prayer.

The crucified and risen Christ will come again, cast out all darkness, and gather His people to His Table as His fellowship. The return of Christ is What We've Been Promised. Christ's return is the Amen, the feast we are headed toward and bear witness to. It is not effort or sorrow but this return that will complete and fulfill us. Christ's return means the only thing more real than the certainty that we've been scattered and lost is the fact that we've been gathered and forgiven. His fellowship is not an objective; it is an inevitability. His fellowship is the Mercy we bear witness to in offering.

The gospel is What's Been Given and What's Been Promised. And what we are going to need in the Wilderness is a simple life with What's Been Given and What's Been Promised, a way to return to What's Been Given and be led toward What's Been Promised.

By His Spirit, Christ is this Way, this return, this leading. Christ is the gospel, and by His Spirit He is also a simple life with His gospel. His Spirit returns us to the hearing of His Word and leads us in prayer to the offering of ourselves to and for His fellowship. His Spirit means He is willing to become our simple life with His gospel, to return us to What We've Been Given and lead us toward What's Been Promised.

We are going to need a way to return and to be led because our trust is a wounded, crying thing. And is in continual need each day, multiple times of day, of being rescued by hearing, led through prayer, and fulfilled in offering. Christ is willing, by His Spirit, to become this Rhythm, this daily procession that rescues, leads, and fulfills our trust. Each day, His Spirit is eager, willing, groaning to return us to His Word and leads us in prayer toward what we offer His fellowship.

His Spirit provides this way, this Thread leading out of the Haunted House through the Wilderness, toward His Table. It is an unbreakable Thread because it rescues, leads, and fulfills the trust by which we hold onto Christ's own indestructible life, a path through the Wilderness secured not by our effort or planning or sorrow but by our involvement in His death, resurrection, and return.

By His Spirit, Christ's death, resurrection, and return becomes our daily procession, an Ordinary Life of Regular Worship. This daily procession is the relationship every day has to the events of Christ. By hearing, through prayer, and in offering, every beautiful, mundane, or sorrowful day becomes involved in the power, promise and peril of Christ's death, resurrection, and return.

THIS RHYTHM, THIS DAILY PROCESSION, this simple life with What's Been Given and What's Been Promised is how the events of Christ become the understanding of the heart.

But it is not just that.

Ordinary Life of Regular Worship is a life of understanding and intention. His Word gives us our understanding; His Spirit leads our intentions. By His Word we understand Christ can be depended on. Through His Spirit we can intend to depend on Christ. By His Word we trust in Christ. Through His Spirit we trust Christ with things. The Christ we can depend on leads us to our dependence on Christ.

Our intention each day is to be rescued by hearing, led through prayer, and to become what we offer. Our intention is to hear, to pray, to offer. Not because it is fun or easy but because it is an inevitability, our life with What's Been Given and What's Been Promised. These three things, hearing, prayer, and offering, are not desires, emotions, passions, skills, talents, or abilities. They are our dependence on Christ. They are simply what we're headed toward. The few things we are being led to by His Spirit.

In a day there may be millions of things we want, a million thoughts we're thinking, a million nightmares to pass through, a million problems leaping out and shouting at us. A billion things we're thinking and feeling. A million things that Could Happen or Should Happen. But there's only a few things we're ever headed toward, being led to. We are always headed toward hearing, headed toward prayer, headed toward offering.

We may not always be able to hear, to pray, or to offer. And we may not have the desire to hear, to pray, or to offer. But we are always headed toward hearing, toward prayer, toward offering. Being led there through His Spirit. Being led by the Christ we depend on toward our dependence on Christ.

Because to depend on Christ is to behold, be patient, bear witness.

To be seen, to be safe, to be fed.

To be rescued, to be led, to be fulfilled.

To hear, to pray, to offer.

Of course we are not changed by activity. We are only changed by Christ, and in all these things we are only headed toward Christ, the Christ we behold by hearing, are patient with through prayer, bear witness to in offering. In all these things we are only being rescued by Christ, led through Christ, fulfilled in Christ. In all these things we are only being led from the Word to Amen along the way. In all these things we are only being led by the Christ we depend on toward our dependence on Christ. In all these things we are only returning to What's Been Given and heading toward What's Been Promised.

There was no way out of the hardness of my heart, and through the screaming Wilderness of body, mind, and soul, other than by being led by that understanding along the narrow Thread of those few simple intentions. Except as my trust was led along this daily procession.

Hear, pray, offer.

Hear, pray, offer.

Hear, pray, offer.

For it is in hearing we learn to pray, and in prayer we learn to offer.

I couldn't live with the intimidation of the mind, the anticipation of the body, and the anguish of the soul except as I became that patient, quiet understanding and those few intentions. That daily procession.

There has been nothing more beautiful and harrowing than having to become that simple understanding and those few intentions. The most important thing in the Wilderness is not to feel better or worse, but to know someone and be headed somewhere.

With the understanding that is the Word of the cross.

With the intentions that are the way of the cross.

The way of the cross is not a skill, an ability, or even a desire. It is the direction of the heart, confirmed by His Spirit. It is an orientation. It is where we're headed, and the willingness to be led there. The only intention given to us by His Spirit is to return to What's Been Given and to be led to What's Been Promised. Through hearing, in prayer, and by offering.

"Is the Thread still there?"

Every morning I wrote those words in my journal. And tried to answer it by living an answer.

I have tried to make my life about following this Thread and not figuring things out, making things right, defending myself, or knowing. I have tried to make my life about heading with Christ toward hearing, prayer, and offering.

Trusting in Christ by hearing.

Trusting Christ with things through prayer.

Entrusting myself to others in offering.

An ordinary life, an ordinary trust, rescued by His Word, led through His Spirit, and fulfilled in and for His fellowship.

Following this Thread, being pulled on by this Thread, being led along this daily procession, is what life is now, what life seems to be about. It's about returning to what's been given and being led toward what's been promised.

With that understanding and those intentions, I have been given a deep and unshakable reverence for Christ that has made it possible to withstand myself and pay attention to others, and to craft a life at various turns beautiful, strange, small, hard, and—even in its anguish—charged with extraordinary means. And I have been able to do it not as someone who is talented or sane but as someone who has had to depend on Christ in order to live. Who has learned to become a patient, quiet man who is finally headed somewhere.

This Rhythm of understanding and intention, this daily procession of hearing, prayer, and offering, was the only Thread that didn't break. In a Wilderness where anything could be seen, felt, done, or taken, and could make body, mind, and soul a Stranger, this was the only thing that was mine. My dependence on Christ was the only thing that couldn't be taken from me. The intention to depend on Christ was the only thing that couldn't be taken from me. This Rhythm, this Ordinary Life of Regular Worship, was the fulfillment of Christ's promise to be with us always, the promise that Christ would never leave us without a way to depend on Him, and that in this way would never leave us with a way to be quietly changed by depending on Him.

There may come a day when because of this awful life we cannot be a good mother, a good father, a CEO, an athlete, or a friend. There may come a day when we cannot be sane or capable, when we cannot be stable. But there will never come a day when we cannot be a Christian. Because a Christian is someone who depends on Christ, who can be quietly changed by depending on Him. We are assured that to depend on Christ is to be given Christ, utterly and completely. If we can depend on Christ with every horrible thing, then in the midst of every horrible thing Christ will give Himself to us, and by giving Himself to us, give us back to ourselves. In this way, even anguish and distress have been a transfiguration. In this way, every moment can be a transfiguration.

A life of understanding and intention is the irrevocable privilege of an ordinary life with Christ, an understanding secured by Word of His death, intention secured by the Spirit of His resurrection. That's what death and resurrection meant. It meant, in a world where anything could be seen, felt, done, or taken, I still got to know someone and head somewhere.

That has been the freedom in the Wilderness of History and Affliction. To be walking down the street and to stop and say,

That is what I'm thinking.

This is what I'm feeling.

But it is not what I understand.

And it is not where I'm headed.

In a world where we can't know What Could Happen, or control What Should Happen, the option was always available to depend on Christ and head toward my dependence on Christ. To trust in Christ and trust Christ with things. To know someone and head somewhere.

BECAUSE OUR TRUST IS SO wounded and selfish, the struggle to say Amen is its own horror. Christ as our cry for Mercy is a kind of horror. It has been an agony to only be that patient, quiet understanding and those few simple intentions. The understanding that Christ can be depended on. The intention to depend on Christ.

This patient, quiet trust, because it grasps the crucified Christ, is itself a crucifixion. In order to get along, to be present in my own life, to worship regularly, to love somewhat well and somehow get through the day, I have been called to enact by Christ a trust that feels like dying. A patient, quiet trust that feels wrong just as often as it feels right. I have learned, and am still learning, that trusting Christ is one of the ugliest and most uncomfortable things we'll ever do. The trust that grasps Christ—even and especially if it is patient and quiet—is a splendid, wounded, trembling, crying thing. We can have this patient, quiet trust and still be upset. We can have it and still be miserable. We can have it and still be in great uncertainty and tension.

This dependence on Christ, this patient, quiet understanding, those few intentions, has only got more trembling and shaky because Christ is being trusted with darker and wilder things and more is being risked by trusting Christ with them. More is being risked by hearing, praying, and offering. But that fierce, bold, pleading, whimpering, patient, quiet trust in Christ has what all our beautiful thoughts and feelings, all our beautiful plans and strategies and effort, do not: all of Christ Himself. Trust is our participation in the reality of Christ. Our death and resurrection is a patient, quiet trust in His. A dependence on His.

Is the path of discipleship, this long, painful move from dependence on self to dependence on Christ that takes a lifetime, still available to someone whose mental illness has not stopped screaming and shouting at them? Whose mind and body will always provide a Wilderness for them?

Is a vibrant, deepening life of faith, hope, and love available to the severely traumatized and the mentally ill? Is a deepening life of faith, hope, and love still available for those who may never feel or get better? Available for those for whom thought and feeling may never return as consolation?

Only, I offer, if we understand faith, hope, and love not as things we think or feel but as the rescue, leading, and fulfillment of our patient, quiet understanding. These three things—faith, hope, and love—are never really distinct. Faith, hope, and love is a trust that has been rescued by His Word, led by His Spirit, and offered to His fellowship.

And we can only have that life of faith, hope, and love if Christ is the rescue, leading, and fulfillment of our trust we have in Him. A trust rescued by His death, led by His resurrection, fulfilled by His return.

The only answer to the intolerable, the unacceptable, the inconsolable is this mystery of faith, a rescue, a leading, and a fulfillment by which even the traumatized and severely mentally ill can still know someone and be quietly changed by heading somewhere. Who, though bereft of thought and feeling, still under the havoc wrought by mind and body, can still live lives of understanding and intention, of Word and Spirit, of death and resurrection. Men and women who have not been so ruined by this life that they cannot become servants and guests of the Mercy offered in His gospel. Trusting in Christ by His Word. Trusting Christ with things through His Spirit. Entrusting themselves to one another as an offering to His fellowship.

Looking intently at a severely mentally ill friend of mine over a cup of coffee, I said quietly to Jesus, "Lord, can he grow, if all he has is trust?"

"Your faith has made you well."

Anyone who can trust can be transfigured.

Anyone who can trust can be rescued, can be led, can be fulfilled. By His Word, through His Spirit, in His fellowship. Anyone who can trust can be seen, and safe, and fed by Christ's death, resurrection, and return.

"WHAT DO I NEED TO be okay?"

I also wrote these words in my journal every morning.

The Word of the cross is always available. The Word of the cross is our trust in Christ. Our understanding.

The way of the cross is always available. The way of the cross is trusting Christ with things. Our intention.

The Word is the Christ we depend on. The way is our dependence on Christ.

That understanding leads to those intentions. Those intentions deepen that understanding.

And these two things are always available. Because His death and resurrection are irrevocable and indestructible.

But are they enough? Is that all we need to be okay? A Christ to depend on and a way to depend on Christ? Can we really make a life out of understanding and intention?

For the longest time all I wanted was to feel okay. Even as I knew it would be a long time before I felt okay.

All I had when body, mind, and soul had become Strangers was the hope that one day a simple trust in Christ would give me back to myself. This trust was a perilous, fragile thing; it cannot be coerced or cajoled. It could only be rescued, led, fulfilled. It was gently rescued, led, and fulfilled by an Ordinary Life of Regular Worship. By understanding and intention. Word and Rhythm. The Thread leading out of the Wilderness.

This Rhythm was a prayer I made with my body. It was how I trusted Christ with what has been taken from me, the mind, body, and soul as I knew them, and how I learned that I could. It was how I did this through His Spirit. This Ordinary Life of Regular Worship was how I trusted Christ with the hysterical Strangers that were body, mind, and soul and how I learned I could. It was how I trusted Christ with what life was like now.

I could not escape History and Affliction. I could neither repress nor correct What's Wrong and What Happened. They had become the screaming Wilderness of mind, body, and soul. History and Affliction have been taken into the body and become the mind's painful, powerful intimidation, the body's cringing, crying anticipation, and the soul's unbearable dissatisfaction.

I could not escape History and Affliction, and Jesus was not the escape of History and Affliction, but by Word, Spirit, and fellowship He was the enduring, the bearing, the overturning of them.

This Rhythm had to be the way not only out of the hardness of my heart but also through the screaming Wilderness of body, mind, and soul. How I made a life with screaming mind, cringing body, howling soul. How I've learned to live with What's Wrong and What Happened and withstand the way they live in me. And to stand with the Howling Boy who endured and endures it.

I simply was not prepared for what the world could do to me, and what I could do to myself.

This Rhythm, then, had to be many things.

The rescue, leading, and fulfillment of my trust in Christ.

My reconciliation with the Howling Boy.

My resistance to the Siren.

The gentle leadership of the Body That Expected the World to End.

The overturning of the verdict.

Because there was a Christ I could depend on, and there was always a way to depend on Christ. Every nightmare, every horror the Siren showed me, every shout and cry from a Body That Expected the World to End had to mean something else. Every good or bad thing now has a relationship to the crucified and risen Christ that changed what it meant to me. Every horrible thing had to be horrible and the deepening of my trust in Christ. Every cry, every shout, every bullying moment had to be a deeper revelation of what Christ would have to be if I was going to be okay. The gaping maw of OCD and trauma had to be the deepening of my faith in Christ rather than the annihilation of myself.

In all these things, there was only one place Christ could lead, toward what Christ would have to be for me if things were going to be okay.

The burial of pride.

The clothing of shame.

The casting out of fear.

The enduring of History.

The bearing of Affliction.

The overturning of condemnation.

The Rhythm, this daily procession, was Christ burying the heart buried by His Word, clothing the shame clothed by His Word, casting out the fear cast out by His Word, the enduring of the History endured by His Word, the bearing of the Afflictions borne by His Word, the overturning of the verdict overturned by His Word. This Rhythm is how Christ bears this life with us, and how we claim Him as all the things we cannot be for ourselves.

And because that is what this Rhythm was, this patient, quiet understanding and those few simple intentions—while also being hard and awful—were also my honor in shame, my courage in fear, my patience in Affliction, my obedience in dread, my consolation in dissatisfaction, my shield in condemnation.

I had to be taught by Christ how to behold, be patient, and bear witness as shame, fear, dread, History and Affliction, the world in all its brokenness and frailty, the devil with all his verdicts and condemnations, was overcome by His death and resurrection and return and not be me. And that my death, resurrection, and return was my dependence on His.

I had to be taught by Christ whether His Mercy was enough. Whether a Word of Mercy was nearer than what could be seen or felt, and more than what could be done or taken. Whether it was true that all I needed in the Wilderness was a Christ to depend on and a way to depend on Christ. Whether it is true that there is nothing that can be seen or felt or done or taken that can turn us into something else. That can keep us from becoming servants and guests of the Mercy offered in His gospel.

I had to be led by that understanding and those intentions toward new expectations. Expectations that were the gradual unbinding of the mind's painful, powerful intimidation and the slow relaxing of the body's cringing, crying anticipation.

I had to wait and see if a simple trust in Christ would give me a soul that was at rest, a mind that could pay attention, a body that could expect joy. A body, mind, and soul that could expect a return to His feast.

WE PROCLAIM THE MYSTERY OF OUR FAITH

The Word, the Way, and the Amen

PART III

AMEN AND EXPECTATION

A YEAR AND A HALF AFTER the worst had happened I went home to see my parents. I had been home since I got out of the psych ward, but it was a different thing this time. My wife and I went together, and when we were there I met someone, a version of myself, a John I hope to meet again. It is important that, before I tell you all the bad things that happened, we meet him.

In the year and a half after the psych ward, I had done a lot of the hard work of getting better. I ate better things. I rode my bike, played basketball, and swam. I went to therapy. And took the pills they gave me. And kept a strict routine so my fragile brain could hobble along with me through the day.

I was trying. I was really trying.

I always liked being home.

I went home to remember what it was like to not be crazy.

It was a long drive, and when I got home, I took a nap. When I take a nap, I usually wake up to find that I have become what I do not understand. Confused, anxious. Ashamed and afraid. I wake up seized by my own desperate, threatened, fearful body. I wake up flinching from the screams of a scattered, shouting mind.

This day I woke up to find that it was quiet in my head, and in my heart, and in the world. It is rarely quiet in all three. And I looked around my bed in awe.

I woke up and I was not tangled up in all the bizarre and upsetting things I could be made to see and feel. My mind had nothing terrible to show me. My body was at rest. And I was simply in my bed with my wife. The sun had come through the window, and I experienced, in simply being in my bed and with my wife, a feeling of such unparalleled freedom that I wanted to cry, suddenly privy to an unimaginable sweetness that I did not think would be my share in this life. I felt, in those few moments, I thought, more joy than I would ever learn to talk about.

I woke up and felt the Lord had laid His Mercy down at my feet while I was sleeping. I knew, on that bed and with my wife and with that sun, that Christ had given Himself to me, wholly and completely. That His Mercy had been laid down at my feet while I was sleeping. It was something I understood.

And now that Jesus had given Himself to me, the body had been broken, the blood had been poured out. And I had been given back to God. I had been given back to myself. I had been given back to others. I had been given back to the moment I was in. And I could finally be where I was.

Mercy held the afternoon out to me: my wife's head on my shoulder, our legs sprawled together, the sun on us both. I had finally met the person I would become: this John, with his wife's head on his shoulder, their legs sprawled together, the sun on him and the sun on her, delivered from the power of sin. No longer bound by the Hardness of the Heart. No longer in the anguish of that unbearable dissatisfaction.

I got to take a good look at him. He was solid and real. He had a sense of humor and a wife and toes. His mind was clear, and he liked to talk. He was gentle, he was curious, he would be at ease even in great distress. He enjoyed the sun. And would live and die as himself and no one else. It was, for being as ordinary as it was, one of the most profoundly religious experiences of my life.

I felt, in all of it, that the Lord had turned His face toward me. And that if the Lord would just turn His face toward me, I would be who I am. And I would be okay.

If the Lord would turn His face toward me, I would be delivered from the Siren. I would be reconciled with the Howling Boy. And I would have a body that could expect good things, I would not have a Body That Expected the World to End.

At that point I had already met the Howling Boy to Whom Mercy Was Offered, but I had been now introduced in this moment to another John, unafraid, and gentle, the Quiet Man in Whom Mercy Was Fulfilled.

At that point, I had become accustomed to an acceptable level of misery. I had accepted a life as someone who always felt bad.

But when I woke up, when Mercy had been laid down, I briefly, suddenly, had all the things I thought I would never have again.

A heart that understood.

A soul at rest.

A mind that could pay attention.

A body that could expect joy.

I thought of verses:

> "Beloved, we are God's children now, and what we will be has not yet appeared; but we know that when he appears we shall be like him, because we shall see him as he is."

> "For you have died, and your life is hidden with Christ in God. When Christ who is your life appears, you will appear with him in glory."

I knew this was the John I was headed toward. A John who would be fixed not by effort or sorrow but by the return of Christ, the John who would be fixed by glory, when Christ comes to say Amen to His own death and resurrection. When Christ said Amen to the Word He'd already spoken.

It was a good day.

I WOULD SOON GO BACK TO an acceptable level of misery. But even misery could not change the fact that I had met this John, that I was now headed toward who I was in Christ. OCD and trauma, History and Affliction, and the way they lived in me could not take everything. History and Affliction, What's Wrong and What Happened, would not swallow me up entirely.

I still had the Word of the cross, a Christ I could depend on. That patient, quiet understanding.

I still had the way of the cross, a way to depend on Christ. Those few simple intentions.

And I would have the joy of the cross. A dependence on Christ that would give me back to God, give me back to others, give my back to myself. Joy is another word for being given back to God, to others, to myself. I could still have the expectation of joy.

Even in a world where anything could be seen, felt, done, or taken, I still got to know someone, I still got to head somewhere, I still got to expect something. History and Affliction would not swallow me entirely. I was myself still. I still got to be myself. A servant and guest of the Mercy offered in the gospel. The Wilderness would not turn me into someone else.

I was headed toward that dependence on Christ, headed toward hearing, prayer, and offering, headed toward the Christ we behold through hearing, the Christ we wait on in prayer, the Christ we serve by offering, the Christ who rescues through hearing, leads in prayer, fulfills by offering, headed toward a heart that understood, a soul at rest, a mind that could pay attention, a body that could expect joy.

And now, waking up from that nap, I'd briefly had it all. For just a few moments, I had been given what I was headed toward.

And it made everything different.

I'd gone to bed with a life that was normal and overwhelming because it was mine, and woken up with a life that was beautiful, simple, and strange because it was Christ's.

Nothing in the room had changed. Everything was the same. But I still felt I woke up in a different painting.

Everything in the room was the same. Nothing had changed. But I still felt like I woke up in a different movie.

Nothing in the world had changed, but I woke up in a different world.

Mercy had changed what the world appeared to me as. The world had been changed by what I understood. No longer a world to be grabbed at or controlled but a world to be listened to, to be prayed for, and above all to be served as Christ served it—that is, by gentleness and by blood, by struggle and sweat and tenderness. It was not to be fixed, managed, controlled. It was to be patiently, quietly transfigured by attention and regard. A world to be transfigured by offering. A world we have been asked to serve so Christ might be revealed. A world we have been asked to offer ourselves to, our offering not a solution or answer but simply a means of revelation, a way to reveal Christ and what He is like.

After, I found myself sitting in the living room while my parents cleaned up in the kitchen. And found myself waiting on something, but what? I thought for a few seconds and realized I was waiting to hear what my parents sounded like. The way they joked and called to each other like little birds. The surprise turn of phrase, the way they noticed each other's day and embroidered on it with constant, happy fighting—their way to build affection. It was theirs to bring the ordinary into the foreground, to look at ordinary things like diamonds. And to do that in their recliners, with their Southern drawl.

I was waiting to hear what they sounded like. And this was nothing I'd ever done.

And while waiting, I was surprised at how still, as a thirty-one-year-old man, knowing my parents loved each other still made me feel safe. And I felt, as I talked and joked with them, that I had finally become a part of things. I was finally a person in a place. We gathered in the living room, sat in the recliner, watched shows I didn't like, and talked about things that were important and things that were not important. At that moment, my parents were not an intrusion on the time I spent thinking. They were not a threat to the time I wanted to spend by myself. They were not a threat to Life as I Would Have It. They were a glory and a mystery, and I was a part of their richly textured and mysterious life. In their recliners with their remotes they had the look of those transfigured. I had been invited into the grace of who they were and who I was.

I wondered at this small moment. My own deep gladness, my ability to really be there. When for so long all I could be was in my head. When for so long I could only be in a screaming body that pulled me away from everything that would ever make me a part of things.

I had found myself, briefly, on the other side of the invisible wall that separated me from my life. Life, with all its tender and irrevocable consolations, had returned to me. The world had been changed by what I understood. By the Mercy that was understood.

I wrote in my journal:

> "To be delivered from my dependence on myself is to gradually be able to pay attention."
>
> "One day I will be able to trust God and pay attention."
>
> "The culmination of all our trust is the ability to pay attention to God, myself, and others."

I felt, looking at my parents, that I finally had what things are. And I began to pray.

"Lord, do not let me lose what things are."

"Lord, do not let me lose what things are."

I WOULD GO BACK TO BEING miserable. I would find, after that day, after that visit, that soul, mind, and body had become Strangers again. Wild, clawing, outrageous things I lived alongside. Standing with them, standing beside them, walking with them would become the work of my life.

I had a brain that didn't work like it should. It was a fragile thing. I had a body that had been radically reorganized by trauma and now always felt threatened. It was a wounded thing. I had a soul that had suffered the Affliction of mind and body and now had a propensity toward its own wild despair. It was a dark, howling, mysterious thing.

I had thought of them as enemies. Their Suffering was a threat. Their intensity was a distraction.

I would have to understand they were not a threat. They were only fragile, wounded, and mysterious. They were only Strangers to me. And I only had to serve them. I was only responsible for serving them.

I would have to offer myself to the mind I had rather than my mind as I would have it. To the body I had rather than my body as I would have it. To the soul I had rather than my soul as I would have it.

I had to slowly learn how to trust Christ with those Strangers, entrust those bewildering Strangers to Christ. I had to slowly learn how to trust Christ with a body this desperate and afraid, a mind this scattered and loud, a soul this broken and upset. I slowly had to learn that these wild, screaming Strangers could be offered to Christ. A screaming mind, a threatened body, a soul in despair could be given back to Christ. And given back through hearing, in prayer, and by offering.

Through Word, Spirit, fellowship.

Through hearing, prayer, offering.

Through beholding, being patient, and bearing witness.

Through returning, waiting, and building.

This Rhythm was how I served those Strangers. And a way that they were given back to me. A way they gradually become companions again. A way they gradually calmed down, relaxed, and joined in my ordinary life in Christ. A way they joined the trust I had in Christ. A way they learned to be seen, to be safe, to be fed. The way body, mind, and soul learned to return to His Word, wait on His Spirit, and build His fellowship.

The Word of the cross, the way of the cross, the joy of the cross had given me the quiet, holy fear I would need to live. It had given me humility, a trust that could be rescued, led, and fulfilled.

The fear of the Lord, that patient, quiet trust, was Christ's most precious gift to me. I'm still in awe of it. In awe, after all this, that it is still there, still growing.

One day I will have a complete dependence on Christ.

A heart that understands.

A soul at rest.

A mind that pays attention.

A body that expects joy.

Until the day they are given back to us, they are simply what we are headed toward. Until that day we only have

Word and understanding.

Way and intention.

Amen and expectation.

The irrevocable privileges of an ordinary life with Christ.

To return to What's Been Given and head toward What's Been Promised.

WE DID NOT BEGIN WITH a heart that offers.

It was my screaming brain, my threatened body, and my soul in despair that awakened my hardness of heart to fix, manage, control, and defend my life.

And it was my screaming brain, my threatened body, and my soul in despair that so clearly revealed that life was not something that could be fixed, managed, controlled, or defended.

I was mad at them for a long time.

My obsession, my fixation, was what these Strangers had taken from me. I was worried that History and Affliction—the Strangers they made of body, mind, and soul—would take from me the life I wanted.

And they did.

I did not want to serve them. I had to forgive them so I could serve them. They had to be released from being what I wanted. When I stopped trying to fix, manage, or control them, I was able to turn my face toward them. Able to turn my face toward those parts of myself. The face I turned to myself was the face I turned to others.

No one begins by offering. No one starts out serving. No one wants to offer. It is something we are forgiven into.

The offer of ourselves is a mystery. A mystery brought on by the forgiveness of sin.

We are given the heart that offers by the hearing of His Word. An offering is consecrated by Word and Spirit. This offering, any real offering, is a mystery born through hearing, led in prayer. But this offering is only the fulfillment of Christ's own offering, an obedience wrought and furnished in us by His. But such small, humbling offerings cannot be commanded or cajoled or coaxed from the earth. This obedience, this dying to self, the extension of the kingdom by the laying down of one's life, cannot be commanded. The Amen can only be the creation of His Word. Only Christ's death can lead us to die with Christ. Not by its inspiration or example but by its own sheer, terrifying power to change you in a place deeper than what we think and how we feel.

Only the Christ we can depend on can lead us to our dependence on Christ. The rich and precious flower of that dependence is our obedience, is what we offer. We depend on Christ through hearing and prayer so that, in its time, a strange and specific obedience might be offered.

And yet, these offerings are the proper end of reverence. The proper end of reverence, of an ordinary life with Christ, of this simple Rhythm, is—through Word and Spirit, by hearing and prayer, by death and resurrection—to become the gracious offer of myself to the world as it is. The gracious offer of myself is a mystery born through hearing, led in prayer, until it becomes what I've laid down.

Such things as service are simply what we have been asked to offer the world so that Christ might be revealed to it, displayed in it. Serving is what we have been asked to offer the world—not so it might be better or worse but so that it might be transfigured.

Embedded within serving and offering is that the world, and ourselves, can only be served. It can only be offered to. Embedded within the word "offering" is repentance, our admission of what we can't be for others, what we can't be for the world, what we can't be for ourselves.

When it turned out I could serve body, mind, and soul, when I admitted what I couldn't be for them, and released them from being what I wanted, I learned what Christ would have to be for me if things were going to be okay. Every time I had to offer my screaming brain, my threatened body, my despairing soul to Christ, I admitted there were things I could not be for them, and learned what Christ would have to be for me for things to be okay.

Not only clothing of my shame, the casting out of my fear, the overturning of accusation, the bearing of History and the enduring of Affliction, and the burial of the Hardness of the Heart but

My composure in distress.

My steadfastness in temptation.

My standing-place in intimidation.

My patience in frustration.

My stillness in anticipation.

My consolation in despair.

My contentment in dissatisfaction.

Body, mind, and soul did not have the future I could provide them. They had the future provided by the forgiveness of sins.

Every deeper revelation of who Christ was was the deeper revelation of who I was, and the revelation was always that I was more limited and vulnerable than I thought. It was always a harrowing and painful revelation of who I was: that there was so little I could do. I could only serve. I could not guarantee

What Should Happen or ever know What Could Happen. And I began to have less and less of an idea of What Should Happen and What Could Happen, but a deeper, more beautiful, and harrowing sense of what I was supposed to offer. Until I got small enough to finally offer what I could.

In this Wilderness, we want weeks that are more good than bad, more happy than sad, more peaceful than turbulent, but above all the struggle each day, each week, is for it to be offered. This life, this little life full of What's Wrong and What Happened, will often be awful, if not for us then for people we love. But it can always be offered. The offered life is always available.

"This day is awful," I once wrote in my journal. "But this day is more than awful. It is also Christ's."

The offered life is the only life that is always available. And it is the only life that is ever enough.

CHRIST HAS DIED

Out of the Realm of Ceaseless Cognition

PART I

GROWING UP AND GETTING WORSE

I'M NOT SURE WHEN I started living in a Haunted House. But I know it was when I was sixteen or seventeen that my ability to think—my sheer capacity to just sit and think—took on the aspect of a physical realm, a country more grand and haunting and tempting than where I was and what I was doing. It was when I was sixteen or seventeen that thinking started feeling like a place I wanted to be.

I was relieved when the present tense had nothing to demand or offer. At an airport, in a traffic jam, or simply while washing dishes or doing chores, and especially when other people were talking, I would simply walk into the great hall of my mind, into a larger country, and be perfectly content for a very long time just thinking. I thought I was a writer so I would turn sentences around in my head like a Rubik's Cube with no solution. I'd stand over the shoulder of the characters I created in the story I was writing and find something more awful and meaningful for them to do. I would come up with interesting thoughts, ideas, opinions, jokes, and turns of phrase, and these opinions and jokes and turns of phrase were friends to me in a way I find it hard to explain, were, in a very real sense, company. How do you tell people that a thought, or a turn of phrase, or a riff, or a melody, or a joke is keeping you company? That it is a real, lovely, vivid, and interesting friend?

My thoughts were my friends, but they made it so I looked out on a different world. When I thought I was a writer, the world would approach me, wrapped in raiment light, as something to write about. When I thought I was really funny, then the world and the people on the street and people I loved, and just about every situation would approach me, wrapped in raiment light, as something to make fun of.

The world could not approach me as it was. The world could only approach me as what I wanted from it. And there was no way to release the world from being what I wanted.

That is the prison of the self: the world has already disfigured itself before you can rise to meet it. Before you open your eyes, the world has already been changed by what you understand.

My thoughts took custody of the world and offered it back to me as something just a little more grotesque, beautiful, meaningful than it actually was. If I went on a trip with people, and something strange or profound happened, I would talk about it until people remembered not what happened but the way I talked about it. And that was something I was proud of.

My thoughts were the closest thing I had to gospel and Pentecost—beautiful, striking, and landing on me like doves.

I trusted them implicitly. They were sight, I thought, and not blindness.

And when my thoughts turned on me, they turned on me with all the power I'd given them over the years, to bless and to curse, to give life and to take it, to anoint and to devour.

I don't know how it all happened. The people I loved most had noticed that—put in a stressful job, trying to finish seminary—my anxiety (which I simply thought was the unfortunate by-product of being intelligent) had got worse. And was getting worse.

I didn't seem to be handling things as well. I was disorganized. Keeping up with school and work, marriage and friends, was first difficult and then impossible, and its being difficult and impossible made me feel bad about myself. A little comment, a critical remark, had a real power to discourage me in a way I had a hard time explaining to people I loved. Advice was condemnation. Criticism was exile. I wasn't hearing things right.

AND THEN, SUDDENLY, THERE WERE all those intrusive thoughts.

I had my first intrusive thought when I was ten years old. I was walking on the road with my dad, saw a big car coming, and thought, "Why not shove him into traffic right now?" The thought—which came, it seemed, out of nowhere, which startled and frightened me precisely because of its unchosenness—left me bereft for days. I tried to make sense of it, tried to understand why I would think that. I eventually cried, ran to my mom and dad, and confessed the thought. And remember my mom saying, "Oh, that happens, just ignore it." And strangely enough, I did. I did ignore it. And it did go away. And it wasn't until about twenty years later that I ever had another.

I don't know how it happened. My therapists said it was the stress of being in ministry while being in seminary, the bad working environment I was in. It was a combination of things. All I know is when intrusive thoughts were brought back into the hall of my mind, I was at first surprised, then concerned, and then, just a little bit later, completely inconsolable. Intrusive thoughts—like the thoughts I had when I was ten—were thoughts I didn't want to have but were somehow there anyway. The content was somehow both intimate and bogus. They did not represent any of the things I wanted to do, were at odds with the commitments I'd made before the face of Almighty God. And yet they made sure they weren't going anywhere.

They arrived like meteors in my waking life. And they wouldn't go away.

The calculus of it, I'd learn, was simple and nasty: because the thoughts were awful, because I did not want to think about them, because I tried to be moral and not think about them, that was why I did think of them. That is why I thought about them all the time.

I would find out later this was a sign of OCD. If the mind is the great hall, the great throne from which you direct your life—I would later tell people—my kind of OCD is when the throne from which you direct your life, that vast country of cognition, is overrun with rats. OCD is a heart and mind adorned with stubborn, strange, and miraculous worries: vivid, utterly compelling, and not true at all. You try to fight them off. But you can't—more rats, idiotic and cunning and crawling over the stupid, helpless look on your face.

It felt like something was now deeply, horribly wrong. My mind, suddenly, was always full of the wrong thoughts. Only the wrong thoughts.

By my mid- to late twenties I'd gotten used to my head telling me stories. My mind felt like a theater I liked. It felt like there was always some kind of film, and that I was way back in the theater with a beret and a cigarette. As weird and wacky as the films were, it always seemed like I was in charge of what was onscreen. My mind showed me what I wanted to see.

With intrusive thoughts it was like I no longer had control of the movie. And it was a really, really bad movie. Lots of jump cuts, no coherency. Lots of things I just didn't want to see anymore. The more I wanted to leave the theater, the more firmly I felt an usher put his hand on my shoulder and say, "No, I'm sorry, but you have to stay." If I complained too much, the usher would make me take a seat up close, so the screen loomed larger and there was nothing else to see or think.

For people with severe forms of this, you feel like there is no such thing as you, there's just this movie. To mix the metaphor, you are not overrun with rats. You are the rats. The rats are you.

You are the symptoms of your illness; you are as horrible as what you've been made to see.

There is something else too, and many with OCD feel it and are too ashamed to admit it. But it is part of the condition. The things onscreen do not just feel like bad things for you to watch. They feel like omens, like things you are about to do and things that are about to happen. You feel a real sense of vertigo, a real sense of sliding, as if you are about to be, without wanting to and especially without meaning to, involved in them. Like you are, unwillingly, about to do them. The screaming warnings of the Siren begin, more and more, to accompany those intrusive thoughts.

Something was deeply wrong.

Something bad was about to happen.

Suddenly something bad was always about to happen.

And with those intrusive thoughts and warnings, you begin to form a terrifying bond with what might happen.

You feel as if you're at the top of a roller coaster, about to dip down into the thoughts and the vision of the future that has been laid out so vividly and perfectly by your haunted brain. You feel like the floor has been pulled out from under you, only you don't fall but are stuck in a permanent terrifying limbo of being always about to fall. And, even though you don't fall and the roller coaster never goes down, and the worst thing doesn't come true, you still feel guilty of all of it. You begin to really and truly hate yourself for what you haven't done but what you're worried you might do, what you're worried you were going to do.

Something is deeply, horribly wrong.

Something bad is about to happen.

And those two feelings—that something is wrong, and that feeling that something bad is about to happen—are themselves something that feels intolerable.

I once wrote in my journal these words to explain it: "There are some people for whom what could be and what could have been strike deeper into the heart than what is and what was."

The anxiety and shame these irrational thoughts and sudden warnings create is tremendous. The content is unspeakable, the peril feels unmentionable, so you make sure you tell no one except those closest and most trusted, and even then you wait with baited breath for the decision they will make as to whether you are still a part of the human family.

Can I be married after thinking and feeling this?

Can I be loved after thinking and feeling this?

And when your family and friends hear you, and accept you, it is so lovely. But then they try to help you explain why the thoughts and feelings aren't rational. And you, yourself, begin to spend all your time making sure these things won't happen. And what's hard is that going into your head and making sure and figuring it out and defending yourself just makes the content more peculiar and the warnings more excruciating. It just makes the Siren scream louder over every part of your life. Until you spend your whole waking life making bad thoughts and feelings go away. Until you are afraid of everything and can't stop thinking. Until your ordinary life is a Haunted House.

And you begin to have important questions: How can a grown man, who loves the Lord, who is working on his second master's degree, be afraid of being in the kitchen? How can a grown man, who works at a church, who writes short stories, who gives his friends advice in coffee shops, be afraid of sitting on a couch with his cat? How can someone this well educated and devoted to Christ be terrified of going to the grocery store to get Doritos?

In response to what it could be made to see by my mind, my body began to crawl into itself. It wouldn't let me eat; it wouldn't follow me anywhere. It was a frightened monster I'd never been introduced to.

One day, it got so bad I called a friend.

"I'm too afraid," I said, "to even watch TV alone. Can you please come over and just sit with me?"

That evening, we were supposed to have a church party on our back lawn. I was supposed to make taco soup and have a bonfire. But instead I texted everyone I knew was coming and told them not to come. And checked myself into the hospital.

CHRIST HAS DIED

Out of the Realm of Ceaseless Cognition

PART II
ENTERING THE PSYCH WARD

I WENT TO THE HOSPITAL BECAUSE the thoughts wounded my heart and terrified my body and because they would not end. The John I met in my thoughts was bizarre and unforgivable. I saw myself doing things in my thoughts that could not be defended or explained, least of all to myself. And, it seemed, the more I tried to scrub off that John, the more he was there and the worse he was, the more bizarre, the more unmentionable.

When we got to the emergency room and told them what was wrong, they put me in a wheelchair. And took me to the place you go when they think you are a threat to yourself and others. It's in the back and to the left.

"This wheelchair," I thought, "is not necessary."

I had to surrender my belongings to a man with an afro and a smile. I put on a gown and was escorted to a room with nothing but a mattress on the floor. It was there I waited, for nurses, for experts, and for the cool breath of sanity to return to me. I told them I was having severe anxiety mixed with intrusive thoughts. I tried to make sure they understood the intrusive thoughts were things I also found disgusting, awful, and did not want to do.

When they asked me what my thoughts were, I made the mistake of telling them. Locked in an empty cell, with only a gown, you feel indebted to whoever comes in. You have nothing real to offer. And so being honest seems like the service you can provide.

I told them my thoughts and how they upset me. The nurses paused. They made sure I knew they were horrified. I'm sure the context didn't help: sitting in a locked room with nothing but a single mattress in the corner and on the floor, bare walls, and nothing on you but a little gown. Trying not to look and sound crazy when that's exactly what you look and sound like.

They went out, came in, went out again. The hospital was packed; they were busy. They began, with their polite mouths and with that look of tired, maternal forbearance, to demand that I understand myself as insane.

They put paperwork in front of a frightened man. They said they were worried I might do something. They made it understood that if I didn't commit myself, they would. If I was committed, it would stay with me. If I signed myself in, no one would ever know.

I thought of all the people who would not know I was in the psych ward if I just signed this sheet of paper. I saw them smiling, going about their day, never knowing I was even here. And I signed that sheet of paper.

They let me have my Bible, a pocket ESV I held in my hand as they wheeled me slowly to the fourth floor, where all the crazies were fed and kept.

"I'm still," I thought, "not sure what this wheelchair is about."

That night I roamed the hallways, devastated, panicking. It was a long hallway with green carpet that I walked back and forth on with my new socks (they gave me socks). Of course the thoughts were worse, catastrophically worse, which made me feel worse. With the intrusive thoughts and perilous feelings there was also now an overwhelming verdict of condemnation. Everything felt loathsome, wrong, excruciating, urgent and hopeless. The intrusive thoughts were all I saw. The warnings were all I felt. This intimidation was all I had. The Siren was all I was.

I had always trusted hospitals, and now a trustworthy institution had told me I was crazy, which made me feel like I was crazy. I was treated like I was dangerous, which made me feel like I was dangerous. I was beset with phantom thoughts and feelings that made me feel evil and unforgivable. It was as if, within a few moments, I had become guilty of everything I would never do and would never want to be.

As I walked around in my ridiculous gown and new socks, I kept saying, "I feel like I've fallen in a well, and I don't know how I got here." My mind, then, was sliding into a teething, spiraling, evil, gripping universe. I was stabbed repeatedly with piercing, blinding lights of excruciating worry: this Affliction was a black hole. It could take away everything. It got to say what everything was. OCD was a gaping maw, a tidal wave lashing my whole cringing body. Pulling me into what I would do to be okay, that vast nest of tangled snakes called the Realm of Ceaseless Cognition.

John, make it right.
Make it right.
Make it right.
Make it right.

John, figure it out.
Figure it out
Figure it out.

John, defend yourself.
Defend yourself,
Defend yourself.

And I remember thinking:

"The worst thing in the world must be to feel this way."

And I remember thinking:

"This is not something I can handle. This cannot be my life."

I was in despair. And what despair was like was this: severe discouragement and unbearable dissatisfaction.

It was a soul that said life is unbearable and I am alone.

A heart that said life is meaningless and intolerable.

"This is not my life."

"This is not my life."

"This is not my life."

"The worst thing in the world must be to feel this way."

Memory is a dangerous place. The Past is humbling and scary. And remembering is an adventure done with great peril. Even as I write and rewrite these lines on my third-year anniversary of having been there, I feel not as if I am simply remembering it. Trauma must be given its due. What Happened lives in the body. Rewriting these lines, rereading these lines, even now, makes me feel like I did when I was there.

I can feel, even now, piercing, disorienting flashes of excruciating, crucifying worry. I can feel, even as I sit here typing this, the certainty that my mind and I are about to shatter. The feeling that my mind and body are going to snuff me out, cross me out. I am reminded, when I go back to that moment in my body—when I go back to when I suffered and suffer again, when I go back to when I lost and lose again—that there was a time when annihilation felt intolerable and inevitable. When things felt both urgent and hopeless.

I have wanted to avoid those feelings since then. I have wanted to avoid the John who felt this way. I would do almost anything to avoid feeling that way. To avoid meeting that John.

To avoid all that pain, confusion, and dissatisfaction. Who can bear the agony of an unmet expectation?

When I meet the Howling Boy, my OCD jumps and tells me things about him. The Siren, of course, never plays fair. It made that John suffer, and now it gets to tell me what his Suffering means. The Siren, always so urgent and excruciating and sure of itself, says that his discouragement and dissatisfaction is intolerable, unsustainable. That his soul's despair makes him unstable. That I could be unstable again.

I've taken, perhaps, a great risk in showing you this John. And have perhaps taken a great risk in seeing him myself. He may frighten you. He still frightens me: the John who is hysterical, walking the halls, wanting to cry and howl.

All of that severe discouragement. All that unbearable dissatisfaction. Feeling now what despair felt like then.

But this John isn't going anywhere. If What Happened lives in the body, the one it happened to has nowhere else to go.

I have wanted to avoid those feelings.

But if I do, I lose the John Who Felt This Way.

And he has nowhere else to go.

It has taken a long time, but he is welcome in my life. He has been called to a Table, to a feast, and he will receive Mercy. He will receive Mercy because he is in need of it. And I have come to take him there.

And so by the shed blood of Jesus Christ I tell the Siren this:

The Howling Boy is not yours.

And he is not mine.

Because he is Christ's.

And I say,

Memory, come back to me.
Howling boy, come back to me.
There is Mercy here, there is Mercy here.

Memory, come back to me.
Howling Boy, come back to me.
I want to see you.
There is Mercy here, there is Mercy here.

Come back to me.
Come back to me.
Come back to me.

I want to see you.
I want to see you.

Provision has been made.
Provision has been made.

Looking back on it now, the reason my OCD got so bad that I was wheeled into the hospital psychiatric unit was the steady lie I had taken on and that had accrued throughout my whole life, that the best way to deal with anything in my life that bothered me, anything I saw or felt or thought that didn't feel right, was to go into my head and make it better, to defend myself and figure it out, to think about it more. If I explained myself correctly and brilliantly to myself, I would think myself into a beautiful place where nothing could get me and where all ugly things would scatter, and an abundant life, free of rats, would present itself to me again.

I would come up with a beautiful, stunning thought. And that great thought, that beautiful, correct insight into my own life, would pull me out of the deep waters and set my feet on beautiful country. There I would be, landing wide-eyed, coughing up water, stunned with what the right thought had announced to me. Which, as I understood it, would always, always, always be reality.

When I finally figured things out in my head, a way forward would present itself in the world.

I see now what I did not see then. There in a gown, walking gently on shoeless feet, and mumbling under the fluorescent lights of the local psych ward, was the life I had made out of thinking more, and thinking better. This was my life in the Realm of Ceaseless Cognition. This is what you become when you only live there.

I would have to face it, sooner or later. My best thinking was how I got here.

I got here by consoling myself. I got here by trying to be okay.

Later, my therapist helped me see it clearly: I had used thoughts as a drug. Like a food addict, or a drug addict, life did not feel right, life simply was not okay, life simply could not be tolerated unless I was thinking. Every problem in my life, everything I met, was an occasion for and was to be managed by Ceaseless Cognition. Every bad and confusing thing was a reason to think more.

And in that psych ward, I had come to that crucial place where such a thing as beautiful, primal, and necessary as thinking had begun to do me serious harm. In the way that such things as beautiful, primal, and necessary as food and medicine and sex can begin to do us serious harm.

And it turns out the only thing that now counts as hope, when you cannot think and you cannot do, the only thing that counts as power is what you can hear. When things get that bad. Life is won, this world overcome, by being spoken to.

What I heard first, very faint, unbelievably small, was a tiny little bit of quiet that opened up in my heart. It was the kind of quiet you find yourself in when things have really and truly ended, when there's no argument left for or against something because it's already been decided. The quiet after you lose the big game. The quiet at the end of a movie. The quiet after you lower the casket in the ground. The kind of thing we mean by "When all is said and done."

There in that hallway it was not like someone had changed the channel in my head but that someone had turned the TV off. The Realm of Ceaseless Cognition was not dimmed or quieted but suddenly canceled, rendered inoperable. And I was not in the far country called the Realm of Ceaseless Cognition. And there were no rats. And it was just me walking down the hallway with no shoes on.

I would begin to understand that quiet as the death of the Son of God. Or, rather, I began to understand that His death was my ability to be quiet, my ability to simply wait. A death that was more than my best or worst day. A death that was more than my heart.

It was just me and the hallway and this quiet.

It was the quiet where I could depend on Christ, the silence after Mercy had been spoken. Because we are not, thank God, what we can think, or what we will do. We are not our thoughts and not even our wills. We are what the Word of God will make of us.

I had just found the Christ I could depend on. I had just picked up the Thread of an ordinary life with Christ.

And suddenly there was something else. And it was not a word, and it was not a voice. It was an understanding in my heart that I should go to bed. And could go to bed. That I could depend on Christ by going to bed. And I did.

I walked to the med station. A kind old nurse gave me the pill that shut off the part of my brain that made me roam the hallways crying. Within twenty minutes I felt better. And I thanked God and I went to bed.

CHRIST HAS DIED

Out of the Realm of Ceaseless Cognition

PART III
LEAVING THE PSYCH WARD

THE PSYCH WARD WAS ONE long hallway, at the beginning of which was the door of the psychiatrist who saw each patient each day. His name was long and foreign. Everyone said he did things quickly, was quick to diagnose, quick to get you doped up and out of the ward. I was new to the floor, meaning I got seen first. They opened the door and called my name and I passed over the line of haggard-looking schizophrenics and attempted suicides I'd eaten eggs with. They didn't look upset about me skipping.

I'm sure they were more than that, more than just schizophrenics and attempted suicides. I'm sure they had interests and names. But it didn't seem like it. It didn't seem like you got to have that here.

I went in.

I only remember the room was full of binders. Not books, binders. Binders everywhere.

The man was older, not quite small, but thin and haggard. His cheeks sunken, eyes bored and knowing. Like he and his patients had worn on each other. My guess was he'd seen many horrible things and was now bothered by very little of it. And he looked at me in my ridiculous little hospital gown, sleepless eyes, and dirty socks. And cast a lazy look over my file.

"Did you have any intention of acting on these thoughts?" He almost laughed when he said it.

I had been sitting there, of course, despondent, humiliated.

But in that moment that cynical psychiatrist had released a beautiful word back into my life: intention. It had not occurred to me, in the midst of everything I was experiencing, that I got to have an intention.

"No."

He paused, looking down at his notepad. I could see that he was doodling. I think he was doodling clouds. He definitely wasn't doodling me. I do not look like clouds.

"You have OCD," he said, doodling. "A few things I'd recommend." He looked up.

"Try not to worry so much. Don't tell nurses what you're thinking. They have no idea what OCD is. You upset them. And one more thing." He looked up again. "Try to develop a sense of humor."

All this spoken with a kind of flat, bemused authenticity, the kind of bored matter-of-factness you get to have because you know what you're talking about.

I took that flat, bemused tone as a word of amnesty. I was being dismissed in the best way possible. I wasn't evil, I wasn't crazy, and I wasn't special. I was harmless and not special. I had an anxiety condition that left me vulnerable to feelings and worries both bizarre and upsetting. I had a profound inability to move on from those thoughts and feelings. And all I needed was to dutifully take an SSRI (selective serotonin reuptake inhibitor) and develop a sense of humor. I needed to go find something to laugh about and never come back.

I was to be sent home stunned and exonerated.

"You worry too much," he said again, looking elsewhere this time. He was getting ready for someone else.

"You worry too much."

"You worry too much."

"You worry too much."

A MONTH OR TWO AFTER I'D gotten out, another therapist told me I wasn't there because I'd had intrusive thoughts. I was there because I trusted them. You could tell I trusted them because I tried to get rid of them, defend myself from them. Kept vigil over them with a wounded and terrified heart.

I wasn't there because I had intrusive thoughts and unwanted feelings. I was there because I found them meaningful.

I wasn't there because I had intrusive thoughts and unwanted feelings. I was there because I tried to make sure they weren't true. I was there because I tried to make them go away.

I got there by consoling myself.

That therapist would try to explain it with his hand. All sorts of people have all sorts of thoughts, sometimes bizarre, violent, intrusive, often involuntary (intrusive thoughts, he said, are normal). He made his fingers flutter across his face to show this. He showed with his hands how thoughts buzz around all of us. He said people with OCD, by trying to avoid or defend themselves from those thoughts, actually grab at those thoughts, those painful, awful stories, and hold them close—and so adorn heart, mind, and body with the haunting, the bizarre, and the unmentionable. The more it upsets them, the closer they hold it; the closer they hold it, the more it upsets them. They are missing the part of their brain that helps them move on. Their life is ruled by thoughts and feelings they can't get over. And in this way a person with OCD is uniquely disposed to hear the unmentionable, the bizarre, and the unlikely as the gospel.

Or, in short, they worry too much.

Of course it didn't feel like I'd been worrying too much. It felt like I'd just been abused by the friend I'd known all my life. Who did everything with me, who kept witness over my life, who kept me company and then suddenly lunged for me, kicked me in the teeth, took on alien and monstrous forms, and shook me like a rag doll.

It didn't feel like I was worrying too much. It felt like the country I'd lived in was overrun. The vast country was now a feast of snakes, tangled, threatening limbs reaching, jaws opening.

It felt like I was being eaten alive by a ferocious new enemy I'd known all my life, and only had a plastic spoon and fork to fend it off with.

The spoon that was my ability to not worry.

And the fork that was that whole sense-of-humor thing I was developing.

How to change my relationship to the friend I'd known my whole life? How to live anywhere else when you've only lived in your mind, only lived right behind your eyes, which is now a place where rats live and breed and want to eat you?

"Try not to worry."

Did they not understand what worry is? That it doesn't feel like something you're doing? That it feels like wolves at the door? That this kind of excruciating worry is an experience provided by the brain? A storm you can't control, an avalanche you stand helpless under? That when they say, "Try not to worry," what they are saying is, "Try not to be eaten by wolves"?

At the time, I couldn't ever remember it happening like this before. Did I have OCD before? How did I not know? How did it bloom in me like this? And by blooming, take everything from me? How could everything be taken from me so suddenly?

But I remember now. I remember I would drive thirteen hours home to see my parents, would drop my bags, kiss my mom who was tired but who had also patiently waited, and then run upstairs to see if I still had all my books lined up in my old bookshelf. Not because I wanted to. I didn't. But because it felt like what had to happen. What should happen. If I didn't then something was missing and I was not okay. The Siren had decided that the most meaningful thing I could do when I got home was not sit next to my mom who had waited all night for me to get home safe, not sit and eat a few of the chocolate oatmeal cookies she'd made and talk with her, this woman who with a single laugh could remind me I'd been loved gently for many years, but to immediately run upstairs and count books that did not matter written by people I did not like. So that my life would feel right, so that things would feel right. My brain could make me get up and leave the people I love most, the people I had driven hours just to see, and willfully choose to sit, wretched and frantic, in a cave full of meaningless papers. My brain, this fragile, terrible friend of unbelievable power.

EVEN AFTER THEY PSYCH WARD decides you aren't that big a deal, aren't a threat to yourself or others, you still have to stay a while. They want to try new meds and see what happens to you.

At the psych ward I tried to sort myself out by walking up and down the one long hallway. Walking down the long hallway was something you could do if you didn't want to watch *Law and Order*. (At the psych ward there are only two choices of what to do between meals: take a shower, watch *Law and Order*.) I would walk around and read the Bible, making those long jaunts down the psych ward hallways.

One day a little old nurse joined me. She made it known by her physical proximity and the gentle look on her face that she was not afraid of me, which means a lot when your hair is all messed up and you can't have things with edges.

She would walk with me down the halls and ask me beautiful, simple questions like, "Tell me about your wife," and "Why do you like the Psalms so much?" and I knew, walking up and down that hallway, that through the pleasant company of this old woman, Christ Himself was ministering to me. And it was more than enough. On a day like that it was an abundance.

I saw her each day, or she saw me. And when she found me, she walked as fast or as slow as I did, down the hall and back.

Being here had been such a profound break with how I understood myself and my life as I understood it. But when I talked, and when I rambled, it was as if she saw the Thread of my life dragging behind me. And when she listened to me, and when she looked at me, it was as if she picked up the Thread of my life and handed it back to me.

I wish I could say I got better because I was resilient and smart. But I got better because they let me keep my Bible and an old woman walked down the hallway with me, asking me very lovely, very simple questions.

I often imagine seeing that woman again, at a mall or at Burger King. I'd like to give her a hug—big man that I am and tiny woman that she was. I'm not a very physically affectionate person. Hugs, touches are brief things. But I'd like to stand there in the mall or at Burger King and hug her for a long time. I'd like to tell her it mattered.

It would be hard to say what it means for someone to turn their face toward you when the world has turned its face from you. It would be hard to say what it was like to be so marked by her company. How I could have been so changed by her regard. What it was like to be transfigured by attention. Vindicated, ratified, unannihilated, uncrossed out. In the psych ward, with my dirty socks, and my unkempt hair, I wore her attention as a crown on my head.

We don't often think of Christ dwelling in hell. But I'm convinced He's there. I'm convinced He's in hell all the time. I'm convinced He pillages hell when we go visit each other. He pillages hell every time we go into the far country to find and see each other in places like that.

And here I had been given His Mercy. It was precious oil on my head. It was good company. It was the harrowing of hell. It was the same as being seen.

I tell people Jesus came into hell to get me, a miracle I count no less radical for being so ordinary, bringing all the power, promise, and peril of His death to bear on this place, not through bread and wine, but through a tattered pocket ESV and the faithfulness of an old woman.

And the frequent visits of an utterly loyal, exhausted wife.

My wife and I could only be together for half an hour at the end of the day. The hour before she arrived I would take a shower and write her notes with the little bendy ink pens they gave you that had ink in them so you could write your wife a letter but were bendy so you couldn't stab anyone. I would wait for her outside the locked door that would slowly reveal her to me after the fat old security guard had checked her things.

We'd walk together to the cafeteria, holding hands. I put my head down on the greasy table where I'd just finished eating green beans, cookies, and burgers with schizophrenics, drug addicts, and attempted suicides (my kind of people, I'd learned).

She stroked my head and read the book of Psalms.

There were about, I'm guessing, forty people in the place where I was. Only I and a young bald man who was angry ever had someone come visit us. I was surrounded by people (mostly poor) who had no one to come see them mumble at a wall, no one to try to help them muster up something small and human in a place like that such as eye contact or holding hands. Something that might make you feel like a person. We cannot forget: we must be seen to be human. That is what it means to be human—to see each other. And there is very little in psych wards that does anything other than degrade the soul, the part of us that must be seen if we are to be human again.

The soul is, again, not something floaty and ethereal. The soul is what we're talking about when we turn our faces to each other and call each other by name.

Mostly no one had visitors.

But for thirty minutes each night my wife would visit me. My sweet baby would sit with me, read psalms to me while I put my head on the table and I tried to only think about what it was like to be touched gently on the back of the head by someone who loved me.

AFTER READING THOSE PSALMS ALL day and talking with that nurse and seeing my wife, at around 9:30 p.m., an attendant would come into the cafeteria with a cart full of graham crackers, vanilla ice cream, and ginger ale. Those three things in that dark cafeteria at 9:30 p.m. was what was known as "a party." I would get my little snacks, and go to the room I shared with a thin old drifter from Memphis, who put rotten bananas in his pillowcase and who snored such sounds as simply were not possible, that have never been duplicated in this world or in any other.

My bed, I thought, was much too small. My feet hung off the end because I'm six foot seven. I would put in my earplugs, and when the light went out I would lift out my hand to touch the wooden bedpost because it was important for me to think that Jesus died on a cross I could touch. A cross I could touch with these big, fumbling, hysterical hands.

I would close my eyes in that room, and it was there that my imagination—a mental world I thought completely occupied by wolves and rats—began to preach the gospel to me. I closed my eyes and saw I was a weary traveler who was very tired and wanted to sleep but that I had to move through some kind of Wilderness up to a clearing where Jesus Christ was, where there were three crosses up on a hill with Jesus silent and dead against a neutral sky, and when I climbed that hill my mind got quieter and quieter because all the wolves and rats—even my most invasive and intrusive thoughts and most perilous feelings—hung back, reverent and aware they could not compete with the solemnity of the occasion.

And I got closer and saw Jesus with His head hung down and His arms relaxed as He settled into His death. He had just finished offering Himself for the life of the world. And I can't explain why I felt so comfortable there, but maybe it was just the simple fact that if He was there, I could be there too. His death was not just being seen. It was a kind of company. It was someone I was with. And I know, because I worked in church and was in seminary, that the death of the Son of God meant many things, but today it meant that it was quiet. It meant I could be quiet.

And I would lie down with the back of my head against the foot of the cross, His dirty dead feet just over my head, and I knew that Jesus Christ was not a beautiful thought or a special feeling because a thought or a feeling could not get stapled to a piece of wood. Mercy wasn't a thought I had to think, or a feeling that had to be felt. It was a Reality that was understood. It was Christ Himself. And what I had, then, was not the feeling of Jesus, or the thought of Jesus, but Christ Himself, and the exact place where the Son of God died.

This death was His Word to us. I did not have a thought or feeling; I had His Word. By that Word He had given Himself to us completely. And I knew that life was not about what was seen, felt, done, or taken because it was always about this instead. It would always be about what was given.

And I knew every thing my mind said and every awful thing it showed me could not take the little, awful peace and quiet given to me by the Word of His death. That understanding was not the same as feeling worse or feeling better. I still felt horrible. And would feel horrible for a long time. Horrible thoughts would abide and abound.

But it was too late. The Word had been spoken. I had been seen. I was with someone. I had been given safe passage. Mercy had been provided.

The Word of the cross and my patient, quiet understanding.

There is found, at the foot of that cross, a solemnity and tenderness found nowhere else. A Word that stands over all time and space, over every History and institution and heartbreak. It is more than what can be done or taken. And yet it is an embrace; it has drawn us close. It is nearer than what can be seen or felt.

It is Christ's tenderness and severity, Christ's authority and embrace. Everything had been dealt with. Everything had been given.

It was the quiet after all was said and done. When Christ died, nothing that could be seen or felt or done or taken got to speak life and death over you. What's Wrong and What Happened didn't get to decide what things were.

The cross is the place where God decided not to look away from us. Here, in Christ, God stared down everything that might frighten or condemn or humiliate us, and to its teething, spilling desire to be the Final Word He has said, "No."

And overturned all verdicts.

And to our wretched, helpless state, He has said, "Yes." And by the death of His Son has

Clothed our shame.

Cast out our fear.

And buried our hardness of heart.

There are things that end at the cross of Christ, and things that begin at the cross of Christ. And that is all there is. There is no future without Mercy. There is only a future provided by Mercy.

Here, with His wounds and His misery was our great need of Mercy. Every horrible thing that can be seen or felt or done or taken was seen and felt and done and taken there.

And here, with that wounded miserable Man, was the Mercy that has been offered. Everything that can be seen or felt or done or taken had become the broken body and the poured out blood of God's own Son, and been made holy that way, had been made holy by its proximity to Him. All Suffering and evil, every intrusive thought and traumatic event, has become the broken body and poured out blood of His own Son. And has been given back to us as the forgiveness of sin.

This was the Word of God, and the most important thing was to hear it. By that Word, Christ had pledged Himself to us forever. Everything had been dealt with. Everything had been given.

And I knew then, in that bed, with that quiet, as my imagination preached the gospel, while I shared a room with a thin old drifter from Memphis, that it's our hearing that God guards most fiercely from His throne. The only trust we have is one that has been rescued through hearing.

It is hearing that establishes us as a relation to Christ. Hearing is our share in His victory over shame, fear, pride, dread. Hearing is our place to stand. Our death and resurrection is a patient, quiet trust in His.

The heart is cleansed by hearing what Christ has done. We are freed from the power of sin by hearing promises. We cannot return to Christ through effort or sorrow, but through the vigilant hearing of the gospel, the Word proclaimed. The hearing of the gospel is the place where Christ offers Himself to us again. Hearing is the place where we behold the face of Christ and are given the miracle of repentance and faith. A repentance that is part of the gift of the gospel and not a condition of it.

It is only hearing that buries the Hardness of the Heart. Only hearing creates the ability to trust the wounded, miserable Man with everything, and ask what He would have us do.

I look and see myself then—tall, thin, pale, scared, and finally able to hear. And see that I was only invincible on that day. Only when I was helpless. Only when my birthright was my nakedness and hearing of the gospel. It was only then that I was ready to storm the gates of hell.

This is a world of great shame and fear and pride. And those are forces too powerful to be overcome by us. There are some things that cannot be defeated by effort, but only by trust. Because they have been overcome by Christ.

The devil is not afraid of the talented and the rich, of the beautiful or the witty or the capable. He is afraid that beggars might hear something. He is afraid of our inheritance. He is afraid of the hearing of the gospel. He is afraid we might hear who Christ is.

LATER, I HAD THE CHANCE to go back to that fourth floor, to visit a friend whose acute schizophrenia was upsetting him again. I was worried going back might be traumatic, that if I went back to the place where everything was taken that it might take more. But I also knew our great need to be seen in a place like that, our great need to let others see us in places like that. To be marked, to anoint each other with the sacrament of presence. To be vindicated and somehow be okay if only by being seen.

Pulling up to the parking lot, I remembered how frightened I was when my wife drove me here a few years ago. And how now I wasn't frightened. Pulling up at that time I thought, "My life is over. This is where my life ends."

Pulling up now, and looking up at the fourth floor where all the crazies are fed and kept, I thought, "That is where I died with Christ."

I understood then, and am still learning to understand, that the fourth floor of the hospital is included in my pronouncement of the gospel, not outside it. The psych ward had become a psalm. The anguish that was here had become a prayer. I had a life in Christ that included coming back here. To speak of Christ was to speak of this place. That is what it would always be.

As I went in, I saw a woman sitting on the floor in her gown, talking quietly to herself. I felt I knew what that was like. Talking quietly to herself, figuring herself out, making insane drawings on the blackboard of her mind, trying to think herself into freedom, trying to think herself into a more beautiful place. I saw how a life spent with a mental illness closes us from the reach of everything except the tenderness and severity of Christ.

I thought of how this is hell for people. Down-and-out people I've met in the psych ward and on the street don't have to be told about hell. Hell is a place they've already been. The question isn't whether hell exists. The question is whether Christ has descended into hell. The question is whether hell is a place He will go to get us.

I REMEMBER THE DAY I LEFT, the day the psychiatrist cleared me, and the social worker set me up with follow-up appointments.

My nurse friend, that old gentle woman with all those beautiful, simple questions, told me she was pushing the paperwork through to get me out. She was worried. She said this was no place for me. She said I would get worse if I stayed here. She said I needed to go home.

The look she gave me was the look of a friend who has been on a journey with you but has gone as far as they can go. She'd helped me cross over. Now she had to go back and help others.

I remember how awful I felt. I remember, even as someone who had just heard the gospel, how awful I felt. I knew who Jesus was and was still miserable. I had been given that patient, quiet trust in Christ, but the thoughts I didn't like and the feelings I didn't want still bothered and hurt me so much, were still so grieving and overwhelming, and were somehow worse now that I believed in Jesus. I kept arguing with them and looking out windows.

I'd been assured that I would be okay. But I told my wife I didn't think I'd ever go home. I was not convinced I just had an anxiety disorder. I was worried there was something more, something deeply and inescapably wrong with me. Something dark and wordless and swallowing and inevitable. There wasn't even a name for that dark, awful thing. But I knew it would be discovered. I simply couldn't imagine leaving or ever being allowed to leave.

And to this fear the Lord spoke, not with words, but with an understanding in my heart. The Lord spoke, not to those thoughts or that feeling, but to that understanding in my heart. I understood something as I walked around and read the Psalms.

Psalms that said things like this:

Out of the deep have I called unto you, O LORD;
    Lord, hear my voice.
O let your ears consider well
    the voice of my supplications. ...

For there is mercy with you;
    therefore you shall be feared.
I wait for the LORD; my soul waits for him;
    in his word is my trust.
My soul waits for the Lord,
    more than watchmen for the morning,
    more than watchmen for the morning.

I read the Psalms and my heart began to understand. And the understanding didn't sound like anything because it wasn't words. But if it did sound like something, it sounded like this: "Stop defending yourself and go home."

I had thought, when I was first in that psych ward, that it was my sanity the Lord had sworn Himself to protect. My thoughts needed to be right, because I was my thoughts. If they were bad, I was bad. If they were heinous, I was heinous. If I had scary feelings, I was scary.

I hadn't considered, and still have a hard time understanding, that my trust is much more precious to him than my sanity, that it honored him more than the feelings I didn't like and the thoughts I couldn't control. My trust was more precious than what I could be made to see and feel.

In the fresh hearing of the gospel, I was not rescued from the appearance and power of awful thoughts and feelings. But only from the trust I had in them. I had been given faith and absolutely nothing else.

What could I do with the trust I had in Christ?

The only thing I could do was not defend myself.

The only thing I could do was not know for sure.

The only thing I could do was not figure things out.

The only thing I could do was not make things right.

That was all I could do with the trust I had in Christ. All I could do was not do something. I only had the freedom to not act, to not engage my compulsions. And not ruminate. All I could do was read Psalms and not go into the Realm of Ceaseless Cognition. All I could do was stand there and trust Jesus and be miserable.

Trust Him with all that pain, confusion, and dissatisfaction.

I would understand later what it meant that that was all I could do. It meant Christ would have to lead the trust I have in Christ. He doesn't just rescue the trust we have in Him, He leads the trust we have in Him.

What could I do with the trust I had in Christ?

What was I supposed to do with it?

Stop defending myself and go home.

In the movie *1917*, a young man, after a blast in an underground mine, is standing there with ash and debris in his face. He is told to jump by a friend on the other side of the chasm. The young man is stunned, blind, terrified. His thoughts tell him not to; his heart tells him not to. His shaking body will not let him. You can see it on his face.

But he jumps anyway. And how does he do it?

He jumps because of what he understands. He does with the trust he has in his friend. What is trust here but the recognition of a voice, the overturning of what we think and how we feel by what we heard?

How did I walk out of the psych ward and back into my life? How was it done? It was certainly not done with the thoughts and the feelings that waged war against me. It was done with the trust I had in Christ. It was only done with a patient, quiet understanding of who Christ is.

Pulled along by something, some promise, a Mercy nearer than what is seen or felt and more than what can be done or taken. Pulled on by a Word that rescues and a Spirit that leads.

It is hard to explain, even to myself. Even the Memory of those feelings is overwhelming. Even just remembering it makes me feel stuck, makes me feel like there is still no way for that John to get out. I look back on that John and don't know how he's going to get out. It is hard to explain, even to myself, how I got out, how I'm going to get out.

But I did. And I do.

I was dragged out by the trust I had in Christ. Led out of the psych ward by that patient, quiet understanding. If this is the work of the Spirit, then the operation of the Holy Spirit is something much more simple and mysterious than I could have ever known. I was miserable. I had no special feelings. It was only that I had an understanding, and with it, a direction to go in. It was only that I was headed somewhere.

I didn't get to figure things out or know for sure. All I got was to know someone and be headed somewhere.

Trust is hard to explain. The heart—the thing that gives and the thing that takes, the thing that offers and the thing that withholds—is not something you get to see or hold in your hand. And yet by it everything else is consecrated: the things we feel, the things we have, the things we see, the things we share. The things we hold in our hand. Our fragile minds. My pale, shaking body.

We always want our thoughts and our hearts to lead our life in Christ. But, as wonderful and as helpful as they are, they are also, until the day of the Lord's return, a snare and a distortion. We cannot ask our thoughts or feelings to confirm or validate those things that can only be known by a wounded and crying trust. It is a simple, quiet trust, born of hearing, that leads our life in Christ. It is the rest that clumsily, awkwardly follows.

"IN THIS YOU REJOICE, THOUGH now for a little while, if necessary, you have been grieved by various trials, so that the tested genuineness of your faith—more precious than gold that perishes though it is tested by fire—may be found to result in praise and glory and honor at the revelation of Jesus Christ."

I've thought about this verse a lot. In 1 Peter there are only two things mentioned as precious: the shed blood of Christ and our trust.

I minister in strange places nowadays. A man walks out of the psychiatric care home that I try to visit now each day. He walks out to a blanket set on the floor, shaking but trusting this little fellowship of prayer that meets on the stoop outside the care home doors. It is scary to him. It is a crisis. But he takes an outstretched hand. His trust makes him sit down. His trust makes him lean forward and try to look at us.

When Christ comes back, what He will use to adorn Himself with, what He will count as precious, the crown He will wear, will be the tested and genuine trust of His people. It is our most precious means of communion with Him. By it we are involved in all the peril, promise, and power of His death and resurrection. What will adorn Christ as His return, what will shimmer off His crown, is the trust of shoeless, crazy people. His great home, His great cathedral, will be the trust of toothless schizophrenics.

"When Christ who is your life appears, you will appear with Him in glory."

How to tell that shaking man that what I see, when his trembling hands join us, is glory? That the glory is not the thought or the feeling but the taking of the outstretched hand? That even a trembling, shaking trust has all of Christ? And when we have gripped Christ with that fragile, shaking thing called trust, we have grasped our own glory and honor? We have grasped the clothing of our shame, the casting out of all fear, the enduring of History and Affliction. We have been seen, and safe, and fed. We have been given back to ourselves, transfigured, miraculous.

And how can I tell it to the man I was? The Howling Boy in the grip of trauma and his own horrific mind? That fragile, shaking man. The man who signed the paperwork, slipped on his old shoes, met his wife at the elevator, leaned on her, and decided to go home.

He doesn't even know.

The Howling Boy doesn't even know.

How do I let him know? How do I let him know that in this moment, this moment that only feels perilous, that he is the safest he's ever been?

Memory, come back to me.

Howling Boy, come back to me.

I want to see you.

I want to let you know.

How can one be sure one is not crazy? How can we be sure that faith is the having of Christ? That faith, even a trembling, shaking, uncertain faith, is the place where man or woman stands transfigured with Christ, even as they are disfigured by an illness? How can we be sure that Christ would never leave us without a way to depend on Him? Without a way to be quietly changed by depending on him, even with an Affliction? How do you trust Christ with an Affliction like this?

And what, with those shaking, trembling hands, did I reach out to Christ for? Perhaps I reached out, still, for my old life, for Life as I Would Have It, my life as someone who thinks. But the Lord, I learned, would not give that life back. I would come out, into the parking lot, into the dirt and sun and cars, as someone who hears. Someone who prays. Someone who offers.

CHRIST IS RISEN

In the Wilderness of History and Affliction

PART I

THE WRONG EXPECTATION

IT IS HARDER TO TALK about getting better. Maybe because getting better is often so heartbreakingly gradual. And the kind of trust that we are going to need—with God, ourselves, and others—in order to even just have an ordinary life after the worst has happened is something won back so slowly and at such great peril. Who can trace the secret Thread of that kind of grace?

When I left the psych ward, I saw a parking lot and cried. I really didn't think I would see a parking lot again. Or sleep in a bed with my wife.

In terms of the symptoms, I came out of the psych ward a lot worse than going in. It is hard to describe how much worse. It was as if my fragile mind and traumatized body had joined into some invisible tentacled monster that had sprung out and held its grip on every part of my life. And I was suddenly afraid of everything I'd never been afraid of.

I was afraid of being with people.

I was afraid of being alone.

I was afraid of becoming discouraged.

I was afraid of having an emotion.

I was afraid of becoming disorganized.

I was afraid of going to the doctor.

I experienced almost every normal thing in life as a profound threat to my sense of self.

My helplessness, which in the psych ward was my great cathedral, the place where I met and received Christ, became, once I left and came home, a stunning indictment against any kind of future.

The Siren had an incredible way of letting me know that every odd experience, every blip on the radar of conscious thought or feeling, every obscure twitch in the self, was somehow darkly meaningful, that there was something dark and awful about just being human. So that

Going outside was reason to be ashamed and afraid.

Driving a car was a reason to be ashamed and afraid.

Seeing beautiful people was a reason to be ashamed and afraid.

Being in the grocery store was a reason to be ashamed and afraid.

A vacation with my wife was a reason to be ashamed and afraid.

The Siren spoke with that incredible and excruciating urgency. It had an incredible way of saying:

"No, John, intrusive thoughts mean something is deeply wrong with you."

"No, John, your discouragement means something is deeply wrong with you."

"No, John, an unpleasant Memory means something is deeply wrong with you."

"No, John, this odd interaction means something is deeply wrong with you."

"No, John, your wild imagination means something is deeply wrong with you."

The Siren, this thing called OCD, didn't invent these things, these memories, these quirks, these embarrassments, but it pretended it knew what they meant. It pretended it knew what things were. It was the thing in my head that got to say what was meaningful. It got first dibs on saying what things were.

Always jumping to conclusions.
The Siren. The Bully. The Accuser.

Always jumping to conclusions.
Always so urgent and sure of itself.
The Siren. The Bully. The Accuser.

All that shame and fear. Droning in my head.
All that shame and fear. Droning in my head.

Something is wrong.
Something is intolerable.
Something bad is about to happen.

All that shame and fear were not simply things inside me. They were the way I saw everything, the way it seemed like everything was about to get me. Experiences, attractions, frustrations, sights, sounds I used to pass by reached out now to grab me. All those pleasant things were now wolves crouching at the door.

When I thought I was a writer, the world would approach me, wrapped in raiment light, as something to write about.

When I thought I was funny, the world would approach me, wrapped in raiment light, as something to make fun of.

And when I had the Siren, the world would approach me, wrapped in raiment light, as something to hide and run from.

I began to understand. Even as I lived and worked and ate and got better, OCD would always be quietly operating in the background, trying to turn the world into what it isn't. It made ordinary life a screeching Wilderness. And it could bestow on this ordinary life a hue of extraordinary anguish.

And now, without compulsions, there was nowhere to hide from it. I had to endure its blast without protection.

I was going to have to make my way through the Wilderness of it without the things I'd used to protect myself. Without knowing for sure, without making it right, without defending myself, without figuring it out, without ever knowing for sure.

When we got home, my wife dragged our mattress down to the living room and laid it on the floor. And it was there that we watched TV together for four days. I couldn't stand anything with violence or action or meanness.

"Can we watch," I said, "a show where things get better?"

We eventually found a travel show where each episode was an extended tour of an exotic hotel. Everyone at the exotic hotel seemed like they knew exactly what they were supposed to do now that they worked at an exotic hotel. They had all agreed on it.

We stayed like that for four days. Through all this, my wife wasn't afraid of me like I was of myself. I don't think I could've made it if she had been.

I wanted to get back into my work and life, and within a few days suddenly, unbelievably, I was—standing there with people in line or at church like I had the same power they had, the same power to work and go home, cook dinner and play. The ability to do that forever.

I went back to school. I could even appear functional. It turned out the world did not end when I went crazy and I could even turn in Hebrew assignments I'd missed. It turned out I could just tell them I was sick.

I worked close to home. Every couple hours I would walk home, lie on the couch, and breathe. And if I wasn't on the couch, I was in the shower, this giant young man folded in a tub while the rest of the world drove around in cars and tried to get things done, letting water run down my head as a constant baptism, closing my eyes, trying to go back in my head to the exact place where Jesus died so I knew I would be okay.

It took about twenty minutes of going back in my mind to the place where Jesus died to give me what I needed for the next couple hours, to drive and smile and say all the things you say when it looks like you're doing fine but when the main thing you're doing is fighting for your life against the relentless accusations of your own mind. Having to always live with the feeling that

Something is wrong.

Something bad is going to happen.

Something is intolerable.

My mind had a special way of making sure I had only those stories in my head that left me without the possibility of Mercy: the assurance I had that everyone would find out I was in the psych ward. The assurance I had that there was some file somewhere out there that said I was a psychotic piece of trash and that a file about me would be released to people I knew or places I would go. The assurance I had that the police were coming any day to lock me up because someone had told them my most recent thoughts. That assurance I had that my wife and I would have to hang our heads and move away.

I had a mind that made sure I only had the stories that made me hate myself. And those stories, those wrong and awful stories, left me very vulnerable to my dependence on myself.

To trying to make sure.

To trying to figure out.

To trying to defend myself.

AT THE TIME, I HAD been going through the ordination process with my diocese. I had gone through the psych evaluation months before my breakdown. I had been told, then, I showed signs of anxiety but that I was otherwise ready to go for full-time ministry. Between that first eval and my follow-up (which was meant to be a formality), I had my breakdown. My psych ward stay had been, of course, kept private from the congregation I served. The lie had been made that I had been sick. The only way my diocese, and this psychologist, would know about my psych ward stay was if I told them.

I had a follow-up meeting with the bishop and diocesan psychologist. I made the decision to tell them. Ultimately, I'm glad I did. But it was a uniquely horrible experience. The Howling Boy is there still, still there with the bishop and psychologist. Still hearing what they told him. It is hard to find that John in Memory and not be humiliated. And to not want to get rid of him. And to not try to restore my dignity now by hating him then.

I pause at this sentence. When I write about this moment it all comes back. I stand at the threshold of remembering: going back to what was taken to have more taken. Going back to when I lost to lose again.

Can Christ be trusted with our humiliations? Can the shed blood of Christ release this Memory from the sealed grip of shame, fear, and pride? Does this Memory belong to the Siren or to me? Can the Siren lose its power to humiliate? So this Memory can stop being a wolf at the door? So that this Memory will not be something that reaches out to swallow me? So that it all can be faced quietly?

So that even these painful memories can be received back as part of my life and not an enemy of it?

Is it really possible for an awful thing like Memory to deepen our life in Christ? For an awful thing like Memory to be a revelation of Christ? For an awful thing like Memory to let us know what Christ will have to be for us if things are going to be okay?

Will the Past ever be anything other than the accumulated witness of repeated humiliations?

Knowing it would effectively ruin my career (and, oh boy, it did), I made the decision to tell them. When they asked how things had got so bad so fast, I said I didn't know. That it had been like falling down a well. When they asked why I checked myself in, I said anxiety; when they asked what kind, I said OCD-related, intrusive thoughts.

I remember the diocesan psychologist as blond haired, polished looking. Nearly young, almost handsome. And kind of nice. But when I said this he leaned in, his eyes narrowed, and he asked me to be specific.

I would then, and in subsequent meetings with this almost handsome psychologist, bear a unique kind of humiliation, that of having to be pointedly descriptive of the content of my intrusive thoughts. Thoughts I had no control over, that represented nothing of the depth and tenderness of my life but were somehow, now, included in the judgment of my character, of who I was. Thoughts that were now treated, by this man, as the prophetic omens of what I might do or who I might become.

I remember it was such a nicer office than the office of the weary psychologist who pardoned me. It was books, not binders. It was family photos, not laminated posters informing you of government guidelines.

But I remember looking at his nice office, the photos of his nice family, and then looking at his shocked face at the mention of my intrusive thoughts. And I knew, by that look, there would be no word of pardon.

The psychologist would make a point to call me that night and make sure I hadn't done anything terrible to myself or anyone else. I didn't know how to assure him I just had OCD and I wasn't psychotic. He called my wife the next day to double-, triple-check that I wasn't dangerous.

Upon proceeding meetings with the psychologist, he would ask me two kinds of questions:

"What kind of intrusive thoughts do you have?"

And

"How many do you have each day, each week?"

Then he would lean in, as if to get tough, as if to get serious: "Are you sure you haven't done or acted on any of these intrusive thoughts?" I couldn't tell if I was supposed to be angry or embarrassed.

The psychologist would then lean back, taking on the air of someone who wanted to be nice but must now preside over difficult matters, and said that, although he appreciated my candor, he "couldn't forget" the disturbing things I had told him. He used his hands to show me what threat level I was now that I had been honest with him, raising a flattened hand from his chest to his forehead.

"Level orange," he said.

"Oh shit," I thought. "Level orange."

The worst fear had come true. Intrusive thoughts meant I was dangerous and unwanted. And now, it wasn't simply an unreasonable fear in my heart. It was the look on that man's face.

He told me my ordination process would be on indefinite probation. If, in a year, I didn't have any more intrusive thoughts, we could begin the ordination process again.

I nodded, somehow penitent and ready to be done, wanting both to stick up for myself and apologize profusely for the way my mind worked. Wanting to hate myself and defend myself. To defend myself by hating myself. To somehow be god by becoming a Stranger to this most broken part of myself.

SUFFERING ISN'T ABOUT PAIN; it's about what gets taken.

The hardest part of having OCD wasn't the actual thoughts, the actual feeling; it was the humiliation. It was the way it took my honor, took my reputation. The unbearable dissatisfaction of having your honor taken, the unbearable dissatisfaction of having your life taken from you.

Suffering is about what gets taken. The way it seems like everything can get taken from you.

It is hard to know what to do with that kind of humiliation, the humiliation of being treated and counted as dangerous when that is so different from how I had ever understood myself or how the world had ever understood me.

I grew up pathologically gentle. I never got in a fight. I noticed when people were sad, and even as a child it mattered to me that they were sad. My mother told me she'd never known a child who tried so hard to make sure they only did the right thing. I avoided cruelty like a disease. I couldn't stand to see people treated badly.

Growing up, I did not mind being thought of as silly, or disorganized, or incapable. I didn't have any particular desire to be rich or successful. But I wanted deeply to be thought of as gentle and kind. That gentleness was the face I turned toward a broken world.

Intrusive thoughts were, then, a humiliation to the way I understood myself. But worse, they were a humiliation to how I wanted to be perceived. I had committed myself to being seen as gentle and kind. And I could not stand not being seen any other way. To have the world turn its face from me when it found out I was not gentle and safe.

Now, it might be said: John, who cares what people think? You know you're gentle and kind.

Even if I knew intrusive thoughts were not meaningful, there were already people who did: the nurses who decided to lock me up, the diocesan psychologist who revoked my ordination. Perception mattered. Their gaze, the way they looked at me, changed my actual life, changed what did or did not happen to me.

Even if I could convince myself they meant nothing, even if I could explain to myself that it was all a misunderstanding and could be easily explained by a very basic understanding of anxiety disorders, there would always be other people who, if they knew, would never look at me and never trust me. I would never be able to control the way people looked at me. And the people who looked at me that way could take something from me, could withhold from me the life I most deeply wanted.

The way people looked at me could take away Life as I Would Have It.

There is a reason people lie. Honesty is a crisis. Vulnerability is a kind of disaster. You really do lose everything when you do the right thing. And you really don't get everything back at the end.

Perhaps you think, then why not lie to those people? Perhaps you might say, alongside the psych ward psychiatrist, "If you had so much to lose, why did you tell them?"

And to this I could only say, the same mind that hated these thoughts also could not tolerate the idea of lying. The Siren that said these thoughts were wrong and awful also said being dishonest about them was wrong and awful. I simply could not tolerate the idea of being a liar. I was caught in the terrifying chokehold of a deeply embedded moral system. A moral system that itself was also embedded in the machinations of OCD. An honest heart ensnared within the Siren.

I both had intrusive thoughts and felt it was my sworn duty to turn myself in. To protect others from who I might be.

After the meeting with the diocesan psychologist, a simple logic fell in place: if it simply was not possible to lie about the intrusive thoughts, and if I wanted to have a life in ministry and to be understood as gentle and safe, and if it was not possible to be ordained if I had those thoughts, then the goal of my life was to have no more intrusive thoughts. I was responsible for making sure the thoughts in my head were not the kind that would upset nurses or diocesan psychologists ever, ever again. Because, even if they meant nothing to me, they now meant something to very important people.

Since intrusive thoughts were a part of my disorder, the most important thing going forward was to make sure I didn't have a mental illness, to make sure I did not have the most upsetting symptoms of this illness. And to come back when I didn't.

To come back when I'd been made clean.

The diocesan psychologist was not reassured that the therapist I had been seeing marked me as no threat to society or myself.

I was, now and indefinitely: code orange. There would always be a question about me.

To quietly and patiently endeavor for the approval of this man, and for the ministry world he represented, was a hideous and pitiful way to live.

It took me a few months to realize, in hearing this, that I had been given a death sentence.

And I can say, now that I have come through so much, and having finally gone back into my head and found some foothold among the rats (intrusive thoughts, urgent, intimidating, perilous feelings), some way to live alongside what my brain is like now, that the single greatest impediment to my recovery was what he said to me—or, better, my sad and quiet trust of what he said, the way I just sat there in his office and heard it, believing that my career, my calling, my life, this call to be a pastor that I'd spent four years in pursuit of, was contingent completely on the mitigation of thoughts that the desire to mitigate could only increase.

If someone was to ask me again how I got this way, how things got this bad, how it took so long to recover, I would say there were of course bad chemicals in the brain, bad circumstances. But over and above this, I had come to believe things that were not true. And the world always changes around what we think is true. It always changes around what we understand.

I was vulnerable to the wrong stories: the story that said I was culpable and responsible for wrong thoughts and wrong feelings, that the wrong thoughts and wrong feelings were something I was called to oversee and control and fix, that said these thoughts and feelings needed me frantically hovering over them, the story that said intrusive thoughts meant I was unstable and scary and that it was my job to make sure I wasn't unstable and scary.

It was a story that made me hate myself. A story that made me hate my own fragile mind. The story that left me vulnerable to my dependence on myself.

If there's something I don't understand in myself or others, it is our deep and abiding commitment to the stories, the relationships, that chew out our hearts and cast us into such deep blindness to ourselves and others. It must be that hating ourselves is still a way we depend on ourselves. A way of clothing our own shame. Casting out our own fear. Enduring our own Afflictions. Saving our own pride. It must be a way that we console ourselves.

It must be that hating yourself seems like some way of getting back what you lost. It must be that hating ourselves seems like a way to make it right. And we want to make it right.

It must be that it is an addiction we can't even see to get rid of.

I wonder a lot about that. I'm afraid there must be something deeply rewarding about hating ourselves. The hatred of myself must be a way my life is still mine.

I REMEMBER KNEELING IN THE SHOWER, just wanting my head to be involved in something other than the terrifying loop of intrusive thoughts and perilous feelings, needing something other than its warnings and commands, saying to myself and God,

"When will the intrusive thoughts go away?"

"When will I be sane and honored?"

"If my mind is showing me things we both hate, and if you can stop them and I cannot stop them, then why are you letting these thoughts happen?"

There were other things the Lord would make abundantly clear. But on the subject of the removal of the intrusive thoughts and perilous feelings that I thought had ruined my life, my sweet friend Jesus Christ was utterly, transfixingly silent. I stood before a wounded Christ who had nothing to say on the matter.

I knew that Christ had died and Christ had risen. I knew that Christ's death and resurrection was not a story. By Word and Spirit, it was ours.

But when would Christ's death and resurrection be the same as feeling better? The same as being sane and honored?

When would Christ's death and resurrection be the same as being stable?

When would Christ's death and resurrection be the same as a career and a good reputation?

When would Christ's death and resurrection be the same as Life as I Would Have It?

Who can bear the agony of an unmet expectation?

After a few months, the vision of the cross I had in the psych ward had lost its power to help me in the way I wanted to be helped. It was no longer something that made me feel better when I felt worse.

Wasn't it, somehow, the cross's job to make me feel better? Especially when, I thought, there wasn't anything worse than feeling this way?

Christ's death was not making me feel better. But I was still fascinated by it.

In the months that marked my recovery, I would color pictures of Jesus Christ. I would find coloring book pictures where He was on the cross. And I bought gel pens, and I would color with them badly. I would sit at home for hours, coloring badly.

Carefully shading his face, his cartoon blood. Without talent. Shading the grain of wood on the cross.

When I did this the questions in my head would dim from all that quiet and persistent coloring and a quiet would open up in my head and the only thing I knew then was not that I was fine or would be fine or that I would get better or that everything would work out, but that Jesus loved me or He would not have done this. He loved me or He would not have offered Himself to me. And this Mercy was not something to be thought or felt. It was a Reality to be understood. Somehow, with those cheap gel pens and in all that pain and confusion and dissatisfaction, I had become what I was, the patient, quiet understanding that Mercy had been offered.

Christ's silence, I would learn again and again, was not His absence. It was the foregrounding of His cross over and against every other pattern and system and category and consolation we have. The silence of Christ is always the foregrounding of His cross. A cross that is the only thing that can be said on the matter.

The cross is always solemn, complete in itself. I would say mocking, but it is not mocking. It stares at us, a confrontation. It can't be judged; it judges. It can't be known; it knows.

It wasn't History or Affliction—or the way they live in us as the body's terror, the mind's screaming, the soul's despair—that would get to decide what things are. It was the cross that would get to decide what things are.

About the time that I began coloring the death of Christ with cheap gel pens, I began drawing in my journal instead of writing in it. There was a comfort in drawing the same thing again and again and again.

It was better for me than trying to find out God's plan for my life.

I could finally, thank God—when I got out my gel pens and started drawing things badly in my journal—stop figuring out God's plan for my life. I could stop trying to figure out when I would be sane and honored.

What I drew in my journal was two hands. Two hands with little triangles in them. The triangles were supposed to be where the nails went through Jesus' hands. And the hands reaching out to me seemed to be all I had. I did not have a plan, and I did not have an answer, and I did not have a story. I had, instead, Christ's gracious offer of Himself. The scarred hands extended still. Extended toward all the pain, all the confusion, all the dissatisfaction.

Scarred hands held out toward the lack of a story.

And when at church I went up to the table where the broken body and poured out blood was held out to us, the old priest's hand with Christ in them, it was not without a certain hesitation toward what was being offered.

What He was offering me, now, seemed strange. It wasn't comfort, and it wasn't answers, and it wasn't relief from the terrible burden of those unwanted thoughts and feelings.

But it was, I saw, a real offering. Something real was still being offered. I was miserable. And Reality was still being offered to me. That was what I understood.

It was as if Jesus said, "I have died, but My death is not done with you. It is finished, but it is not finished with you. Here, have more of My death."

And yet I had no clue what His death would do to me, what kind of joy and anguish and clarity and confusion His death would bring.

Despite all of the pain, confusion, and dissatisfaction, I still knew when I looked at the cross, I was staring at His provision. Here, all that God could do was done. All that God could say was said. All that God could give was given. Here, in this place and in this way, God had been abundant with us. Here is where He would always be abundant.

"Here, here, is what you need."

The gracious offer of Himself.

The gracious offer of Himself.

The gracious offer of Himself.

I didn't exactly know what I was looking at, but I knew at least I was looking, blindly staring, at His decision to not turn His face from us.

Here at least I knew I was being seen and fed. I had turned my face to the God who would not turn His face from me.

I was miserable.

I had the mind's screaming, the body's terror, the soul's despair.

But I still had the anointing.

I still had the heart's understanding.

The trust in Christ that was myself.

The worst had happened, and I was still myself.

WHEN I TOOK THE BROKEN BODY, and the poured out blood, when I took the Word, I was given the burial of my hardness of heart, and provision for the soul's unbearable dissatisfaction.

We would like for our life in Christ to remove the things that disturb and reveal and frighten us, the Pasts that confuse and disorient our present.

Problems make us look for solutions; questions make us search for answers. Diseases make us search for cures. Illnesses make us search for healing. Tension makes us look for relief. Feeling worse makes us look for ways to feel better.

What is the logic of Mercy if it does not follow this pattern? It must be that Mercy is a strange business.

What do we do when Mercy is no longer presented to us as things getting better? When our life in Christ presents itself to us as things getting worse, things getting more disturbing, more revealing, more frightening? When our life in Christ presents itself to us as scary questions and complete bewilderment?

What was I to make of the Mercy offered in the gospel, Christ's enormous and enigmatic offer of Himself—if it was not solutions to problems, answers to questions, cures for diseases, healing for illnesses? Better thoughts for worse thoughts? Good feelings for bad feelings?

And those questions being met with nothing but the silent and solemn figure of Christ Himself.

We would rather not have Mercy if Mercy doesn't get to mean what we want it to mean. We would rather, it seems, not have Mercy if what Mercy means is a crucifixion. There is little, it seems, we can do with a crucifixion. We would like, perhaps, for Christ to offer something other than what He offered.

It is hard to tell people, and it is hard to believe myself, that when we are that miserable and when we feel that bad, Christ has not gone further away but nearer, that if Christ's salvation is as far as the curse is found, then it must work its way into the wounded, selfish heart of men and women who hold their lies very close, so close they do not think they are holding them at all, and lies so dear they do not seem like they are lies at all, sins so fundamental to their perception of themselves that they do not seem like sin at all. And the reason they do not seem like lies at all and the reason we do not see them at all is because we do not understand, we are not able to understand, our field of perception itself is a distortion.

This, as far as I can tell, is sin. Sin is not, ultimately, a thought or a feeling or act. Sin is perspective, it is a way of looking at things, it is what things are to us. Sin is like that Siren. It is always quietly working in the background, turning the world into what it isn't.

Sin is not a thought or feeling.

Sin is a lie.

Sin is a bad expectation.

In order for Christ to come to us there, to meet us in that place, it must be through a special kind of revelation. It must be that Christ has come to us as our wounded, crying need of Him, as what He will have to be for things to be okay.

It must be that Christ has become our cry for Mercy. It must be that Christ has become the groaning too deep for words.

When we do not see Christ working, or do not understand how He is working, or don't really think that He is working with us or in us at all, we forget that our understanding, our thoughts and feelings, our perceptions and wisdom on the matter, our discernment, our way of looking at things is continually and always in the process of being cast down by the cross of Christ. Gradually being undone by the hearing of that Word.

A Mercy that becomes our cry for Mercy.

Why do we think we will perceive and understand what Christ is doing, with perceptions and understanding that are being cast down by His cross?

When we perceive Christ has gone silent, that He is no longer working within paradigms we had heretofore understood or shook hands and agreed on when we became Christians, it is not because Christ has left but because He has drawn near. He is nearer than what can be thought or felt. Christ is as near as the deepest lie. Christ is as near as what we understand. Which is why a life with Christ can be so unexpected and so painful. Who can bear to have Christ as near as the deepest lie?

What can bear the agony of a ruined expectation?

What kind of Mercy is this? What kind of Mercy becomes the cry for Mercy?

Is there really something worse than all this shame and fear?

Is there really something worse than feeling this way?

Is there really a lie so deep and convincing that it is worse than feeling this way? Worse than all this shame and fear?

IS THERE REALLY A LIE so deep and convincing that it is worse than feeling this way?

And what is that lie? What is the deepest lie?

The worst lie, the worst story I can think of, is the lie that says my life is mine and that there is such a thing as Life as I Would Have It.

That is the only expectation that must be undone. And it is the longest, cruelest agony of the Christian life. But it must be undone.

Because it is by way of that lie that I have held most fiercely and closely to my dependence on myself. And nothing has disfigured me more than my dependence on myself. The lie that I can depend on myself is the only thing that has truly ruined me, the only that thing has turned me into something else.

I've said it before. I've said a lot of things before, and keep saying them. To you, to me, to who I'll be when I look back at this.

We are not most changed by what we think or feel or by what happened. We are most changed by what we depend on. And nothing has disfigured me more cruelly than my dependence on myself.

Nothing has more powerfully manifested my compulsion to depend on myself than my long sojourn in the Realm of Ceaseless Cognition. Than knowing for sure, making things right, defending myself, figuring things out.

I would look again at the cross. The cross that had once powerfully, and now intermittently, rendered inoperable the Realm of Ceaseless Cognition. That had somehow given me, even while the Siren screamed—even while I was devoured by rats and wolves called What Could Happen and What Should Happen—that patient, quiet understanding. That there was nothing I needed to do to be okay.

There was a tenderness and severity to His cross, His silence. The cross that was both His death and my patient, quiet understanding.

The anointing. That patient, quiet understanding.

We were not going to answer the questions I drew on the maniacal blackboard of my mind, Christ told me with His silence. They were the questions born of a vicious administration called Life as I Would Have It.

The hardness of my heart is a thing called Life as I Would Have It.

He had come to offer Himself to me and to do stunning and terrifying and irreparable damage to Life as I Would Have It.

Not because He doesn't like me.

Or because He doesn't love me.

Because there was no such thing.

Because Life as I Would Have It is a snare and delusion.

Because in a Wilderness of History and Affliction, where anything can be seen, felt, done, or taken, there is no way to hold on to What Should Happen, or know What Could Happen.

A Life as I Would Have It, a life spent securing What Should Happen, finding out What Could Happen, is a life spent depending on myself. Because we cannot ever perfectly secure What Should Happen, or find out What Could Happen, Life as I Would Have it would always be a life of fear and shame.

Christ had clothed my shame, cast out my fear.

But only because He had buried Life as I Would Have It.

Christ would clothe the shame clothed by His Word.

Cast out the fear cast out by His Word.

But only as we made our way out of Life as I Would Have It.

This was what I understood by His silence. This was my patient, quiet understanding.

I was to walk with Him, during those months of painful and inexplicable silence. I was to patiently bear the yoke of better questions.

The Lord had not committed Himself to my plans. The Lord had committed Himself to me. Learning the difference was what was to make up the long arc of the Christian life.

I BEGAN TO KEEP A SMALL Bible in my back pocket. At coffee shops or in traffic or while walking around I began to read the Gospel of Mark. The Gospel of Mark is as close as Christ comes to being in an action film, of being a comic book character. It's a Gospel made up, not of a teaching or theology, but of appearances, of simple, beautiful, disturbing things Christ did. Things left unadorned, unexplained.

And they were pictures in the hall of my mind. They were not the answer to anything. They were not going to help me figure things out. Or make things right. Or defend myself. That was not their function. They were to be looked at, these little Gospel stories, these little icons, hung high up on the mantle of a mind full of rats and wolves.

Even as I was devoured by the wolves and rats, assaulted with What Could Happen, and What Should Happen, I headed toward the spooky Christ beheld in the Gospel of Mark.

The Gospel of Mark was something I could pay attention to even when I was miserable. I could have all that pain, confusion, and dissatisfaction and still read the Gospel of Mark.

Hearing those stories wasn't like learning about Christ. It was like being regarded by Christ. Reading the stories again and again was like having Christ take a good, long look at you. And to be healed as you were seen by Him. Healed in some deeper place than what you thought or felt. Healed by what you understood. Changed by who He is.

The story in the Gospel of Mark that meant the most to me was the story of Jesus in a boat in a storm. The storm is raging; the water is piling in. The ship is sinking. The disciples are overwhelmed, overwrought.

They yell for Jesus, who is sleeping, but who then gets up and silences the waters, and asks the disciples why they didn't trust him. And all of a sudden the question that matters is not the boat or the storm but, Who is this guy?

I could picture myself, with all these intrusive thoughts and perilous feelings, in that boat. The Siren, and this Body That Expected the World to End, made ordinary life feel like drowning. Made it always feel like being about to drown. Like everything was always wrong, like everything was always about to crash in.

Something is wrong.

Something is intolerable.

Something bad is about to happen.

The excruciating, stabbing worry. The feeling of being pulled into the worst that can possibly happen.

The terror of annihilation, a violent, trembling thing in my body.

I'm in that boat and I'm bailing out water. I'm making sure. I'm defending myself. I'm figuring things out. I'm making things right.

And I'm in that boat with Christ and His silence.

And in that boat and with that silence, it was as if Jesus had said, "What are you doing?"

I've said it before. It was not obvious, and I still by and large had a hard time understanding that with all I was experiencing that there was still something I was doing.

That I got to have an intention.

"I'm trying to defend myself. I'm trying to make these things go away so I can live."

"Who told you to defend yourself?"

"But I'm responsible. I'm responsible for the wrong thoughts, and the wrong feelings. I'm responsible for them. I'm responsible for them. I'm responsible for figuring them out, for making sure I know what they mean. I'm responsible for making sure I have the right thoughts and feelings."

And in that boat, if the Lord's silence had something to say, it was

"Why?"

"Why?"

"Why?"

"Why do you need to have the right thoughts and the right feelings?"

"So that I'll be okay."

"So that I'll be okay."

"So that I'll be okay."

"So that I'll be okay."

"So that I'll be okay."

"I need to have the right thoughts and the right feelings so I'll be okay. Because that's what life is. Life is a bunch of stuff you have to figure out so you'll be okay."

And in that boat, Christ's silence says,

"What do you need to be okay?"

"What do you need to be okay?"

"What do you need to be okay?"

"What do you need to be okay?"
"What do you need to be okay?"
"What do you need to be okay?"

"I need to not have these terrible thoughts, terrible feelings."

"Why?"

"Because that is what I am."
"That is what I am."
"That is what I am."
"I am all these terrible thoughts and feelings."

Christ's silence says, "That is what you are experiencing. That is the flood coming in. And the wind all around you."

And then His silence says,

"Who are you?"
"Who are you?"
"Who are you?"

And I understand. I am not the wind or the rain. I am the one in the boat.

I am the one in the boat. I am the one frantically bailing out water, the one frantically rocking the boat.

And we sit in that boat, drowning, and Christ's silence says,

"John, what are you doing?"
"John, what are you doing?"
"John, what are you doing?"

I could feel the water going up and in my mouth. So many terrible, urgent worries. So many terrible, awful things almost about to happen.

"John, what are you doing?"

"John, what are you doing?"

"John, what are you doing?"

I am consoling myself.

That is what we are always doing.

We are always doing what we think we need to do to be okay. That is what we are always doing.

And I stop. And I understand.

It's not our experiences that are killing us; it's our consolations.

My thoughts and feelings were not killing me. My desire to control them was killing me.

I could only be killed by Life as I Would Have It.

And I stop. I understand. The wind still howls. The rain still comes in. But we are not sinking. I have become that patient, quiet understanding.

What were the disciples supposed to do?

They were supposed to feel that peril, that sensation of drowning, and look to Christ. They were supposed to wait on Christ to speak. They were supposed to point themselves toward the silent Christ. They were to be changed by the Mercy they waited on. The Mercy who looked at them and said,

"Don't you trust me?"

"Don't you trust me?"

"Don't you trust me?"

"Don't you trust me?"

In trying to avoid those dark and awful thoughts, I had only handed myself over to the Realm of Ceaseless Cognition. In trying to avoid sin, I had only increased the power of sin. And the power of sin was my dependence on myself.

And to that compulsion, that urge

To make sure.

To make right.

To defend myself.

To know for sure.

To be responsible.

Christ's silence said,

"Behold."

"Behold."

"Behold who Christ is."

And so, in the face of horrible intrusive thoughts and horrific feelings, I had been given an extraordinary choice.

To defend myself,

Or to be with Christ.

To fix it,

Or to be with Christ.

To make it right,

Or to be with Christ.

To be moral,

Or to be with Christ.

To make myself clean,

Or to behold the face of Christ.

These thoughts and feelings had made me so sad, and I had tried so hard to get rid of them.

Is it enough to be sad? And to try harder? Can effort or sorrow create the future? Will effort or sorrow give the world back to us?

I already knew.

Mercy provides the future.

And we, the fragile and unseen and insane, cannot create the future by effort or sorrow but only as we behold His Mercy with fear and trembling. And become those to whom Mercy has been offered. Servants and guests of the Mercy that has been offered.

Our first priority is not to defeat sin but to behold the Christ who has defeated sin.

If we are going to live, if we are going to have any way through, any way forward, we are going to need something that is not effort or sorrow but the beholding and the following and the serving of Another. The One who is Mercy and whose Mercy rescues, whose Mercy leads, and whose Mercy fulfills.

I knew somehow and in some slow way that Jesus and I would walk out of the Haunted House, out through this Wilderness of rats and wolves, bad thoughts and urgent feelings, but only by His Mercy, by His voice, and at His pace, even as I limped and howled for all these things to just be gone.

And when Christ did come to me, and speak to me, and break His silence, it was not in fresh, ecstatic revelations but in plain words already spoken. Not with special things for me but with things he'd told all of us. His Word in the Scripture. The genius, the compassion of Christ is His patient willingness to approach us again—and to do new work in the heart—through what he's already said and what he's already done.

I read and reread and reread the Gospel of Mark so that Christ would find me. To hear with faith so that I might see the face of Christ and be changed by who He is.

"Follow me," He said.

"The kingdom of God is at hand," He said.

"Repent and believe the gospel," He said.

And with each plainspoken turn of phrase, it was as if Jesus had said,

"Life is not what you thought it was."

"It is richer, more haunting, more strange and awful and joyful. In ways you are just now learning to talk about it."

"And life, this life, is Stranger, simpler, harder, and more beautiful than anything you can see or hear or know or think of yourself."

"Because life is not a bunch of stuff to figure out. Life is not What Should Happen or What Could Happen. It is not the mind's intimidation or the body's anticipation. Life is Someone you are with. And I am the Someone you are with."

When I read, I didn't know if my thoughts or feelings would ever return to me as consolation ever again. If body, mind, and soul would ever stop being screaming Strangers. But I was learning I did not need them to. I did not need the right thoughts and the right feelings to be okay.

I needed Christ to be okay. And I only had Christ by trust.

I only needed trust to be okay.

This patient, quiet, shaking trust was really all I had. But by it I had all of Christ.

If I had Mercy, I had the cry for Mercy. If I had the cry for Mercy, I had the Mercy that had been offered.

And Christ and I were headed somewhere. Christ and I were headed in this Wilderness toward my dependence on Christ.

THE GOSPEL OF MARK WAS a turning point for me.

There was only one way I had left the psych ward, by simple trust in the Lord's Mercy. And there was only way I would live, by simple trust in the Lord's Mercy.

The question, though, remained.

How do you do that?

What was I supposed to do with the trust I had in Christ? What kind of things are you supposed to do with the trust you have in Christ?

How would Christ like to be trusted?

If Ceaseless Cognition was what I did with the trust I had in myself, then what was I supposed to do with the trust I had in Christ? What was I supposed to do with that patient, quiet understanding?

Just stand here and cry? And have extraordinary visions in psych wards? And stand under the shower and wait to feel better?

How was I supposed to make a life out of that patient, quiet understanding? How could a simple trust in Christ be both deepened and expressed in a broken, ordinary world? What else could be done with a trust that has been rescued by hearing?

If defending myself, and figuring things out, and making things right were how I depended on myself, then how was I supposed to depend on this guy the rest of my life?

And how had Christians done it throughout the centuries?

It took a long time. And I did not learn it all at once. But I began to learn that an Ordinary Life of Regular Worship was what I could do with the trust I had in Christ. It was how Christians had depended on Christ for thousands of years, and more importantly how Christ could be depended on.

And that Ordinary Life of Regular Worship was three things. One of which I already knew.

It was hearing.

It was prayer.

It was offering.

These are the ways we are with Christ: by hearing, through prayer, in offering. These are the ways Christ is with us.

Hearing, prayer, and offering, by His Word, through His Spirit, in His fellowship.

But it was not immediately obvious that this was the Thread. It was not obvious that I could depend on the person of Christ by hearing, through prayer, in offering. And that Christ would rescue, lead, and fulfill that trust by hearing, through prayer, in offering.

It all seemed kinda stupid.

It was not immediately obvious how I could consistently put my trust in anything other than what I was thinking and how I was feeling. It was not immediately obvious that I could consistently put my trust in anything other than the Siren and a Body That Expected the World to End. It was not immediately obvious that I could put my trust in anything other than the soul's unbearable dissatisfaction. Particularly because what I was thinking and how I was feeling was so vivid and turbulent and powerful it did not seem like there was anything other than that turbulence.

Again, it did not seem possible, in the midst of that storm, that I still got to have an intention. That, in the midst of everything I was experiencing, in the midst of all the vivid and horrible experiences provided by body, mind, and soul, there could be something I was doing. Something I could consistently, slowly, ploddingly intend to do.

It did not seem possible that the Thread was always there, that this Thread of my dependence on Christ was always there and that Christ was always leading me along there.

It didn't really seem true that if I could trust, then I got to have an intention. That those intentions were mine, secured by

Word and Spirit, by death and resurrection. And these were my intentions: hear, pray, offer. Hear, pray, offer. Hear, pray, offer.

It didn't seem true that I got to have Christ, not by thought or by feeling or by ability, but by intention. That is how I got to have Christ. If my intention was to be with Christ, then I was with Christ.

It took a while to learn this.

It was not immediately obvious that by Word and Spirit, understanding and intention, I would be so deeply connected to Christ Himself, the Christ who is our only consolation. That hearing, prayer, and offering would become the beholding, and the following, and the serving of the Mercy offered in the gospel.

That an Ordinary Life of Regular Worship was the rescue, and the leading, and the fulfilling of the patient, quiet trust that seemed to be who I was.

That if Ceaseless Cognition was how I made a life with the Siren, then hearing, prayer, and offering were how I would make a life with Christ. How I could live simply and vulnerably and with Christ.

That they were the things I could do when I was scared and miserable, how I took hold of the Thread leading out of the Haunted House of shame and fear and pride and into my new life.

It was not immediately obvious that, faced still with the stupefying power of intrusive thoughts and perilous feelings, all we can do is patiently follow the narrow Thread of our intentions. And hope to be quietly changed by heading somewhere.

Into my dependence on Christ.

Into the future provided by Mercy.

Like I said, it took a while. It took years. It will take a while. It will take a lifetime.

And while it happened, I was still mentally ill. While it happens, I am still mentally ill.

I had said it before, that this patient, quiet trust was not the removal of my illness or its symptoms—the urgent, perilous feelings or the horrible thoughts. With these new intentions I still could not litigate against their appearance, or mitigate their intensity.

But I *was* gradually, painfully rescued from the need to defend myself from them. To control them. I could, with these new intentions, instead become a sojourner who passed through them *on his way somewhere else*. A sojourner slowly becoming a servant and guest of the Mercy offered in the gospel.

Sometimes following this Thread was a joy, a deep pleasure. But often it was an itchy, scratchy new yoke, the painful contracting of the self. Learning a life as a smaller thing. Abiding each moment, moment by moment. Becoming a hard kernel, a small boat, a single hot coal, a small foothold in the experiences provided by body, mind, and soul.

Becoming not someone who fixes, or someone who controls. Someone who manages Life as I Would Have It.

But someone who hears, someone who prays, someone who offers.

YES, BUT WHAT DID IT look like?

It looked like a schedule, a pattern, a routine, a Rhythm.

The Lord Jesus Christ, who bore my sins and carried my sorrows, gave me visions and regarded me with His silence, came down off the cross and gave me a Rhythm. The Christ I could depend on came down and gave me a way to depend on Christ. An Ordinary Life of Regular Worship.

A Rhythm that was my friendship with Him. A Rhythm that was Christ's rescue, leading, and fulfillment of the trust I had in Him.

It is perhaps fitting that since so much of our life is made up of unhealthy habits, Christ would befriend us through patterns. And make His way into the human heart through patterns. To carve understandings in that place and in that way.

This Rhythm was how I trusted Christ with my ordinary life. This Rhythm was how I took hold of the Thread. How I took hold of Christ's death, resurrection, and return. Or, alternately, how Christ's own life took hold of mine. It was a rope I pulled on, and a rope that pulled on me.

It can be hard to say what a Rhythm means, how a regular mealtime, a regular time of prayer, any still point outside of how we think and feel, is a kind of friend, a kind of company. And that we need those more than thoughts or feelings. Because to only have what we think and what we feel is to be really and truly alone.

This Rhythm was a friend, older and wiser than I was, generous with me when I wasn't, and less easily deceived. By this Rhythm I was led out of the snares and delusions of Life as I Would Have It, led out of the vicious regime of self-regard, and out of the Realm of Ceaseless Cognition. Keeping it was the taking of the outstretched hand. It helped me move on from obsessive thoughts and walk right past perilous feelings. It provided me with the transitions that my brain couldn't.

It was my resistance to the Siren.

And my reconciliation with the Howling Boy.

And the gentle leadership of a Body That Expected the World to End.

What kind of life is possible with these three Strangers: the mind's screaming, the body's terror, and the soul's despair?

A simple life with the Christ who died, the Christ who's risen, the Christ who'll come again.

A life of understanding and intention: that patient understanding, those diligent intentions, slowly leading body, mind, and soul to new expectations and proper longings.

An Ordinary Life of Regular Worship, a simple life with a trust that could be rescued, led, and fulfilled, offered me the future that my thoughts and feelings and despair would not. It became a miracle: a way forward when there was no way forward.

And it helped me understand, helped me understand that there was a Thread through every beautiful, dull, horrible moment. Through an Ordinary Life of Regular Worship I slowly began to understand that every beautiful, dull, horrible moment was one in which Christ could be depended on. And that every beautiful, dull, horrible thing could deepen our life in Christ.

Without even wanting or meaning to.

CHRIST
IS
RISEN

In the Wilderness of History and Affliction

PART II
THE ORDINARY LIFE

THE RHYTHM I KEPT WAS called the Daily Office. It comes out of the Anglican tradition.

The Daily Office is a set of four worship services you can do with others or by yourself throughout the day. With each service, Scriptures are read, prayers are spoken, and that portion of the day (morning, midday, evening, and before bed) is offered to Christ. More than anything, it is a way to trust in Christ and trust Christ with your day. To cultivate understanding and intention.

I tried to do the four services each day, most of the time I did three, I almost always did two (morning and evening), and made it a priority to at least do Morning Prayer. Most importantly, it was something I could even do when I was miserable. It was something I could do with all the pain, confusion, and dissatisfaction. It was a way that I knew, even with all the confusion and chaos of mental illness and trauma, that I still had a self, even though miserable and small, a self that I could hand over (and even when I couldn't, at least, intend to hand over) to the hearing of His Word, to prayer in His Spirit and to the offering of Myself to His fellowship.

I would wake up every day in what can only be described as a BFM (Bad F—— Mood). It was that brief and intense combination of both urgency and hopelessness. A sudden revolt of grief and despair. And a head full of hot garbage. Previously I had always believed the BFM was a sign that I just wasn't a morning person. For most of my life the BFM was a harbinger of absolutely nothing, except that I maybe needed a sandwich. But now my OCD, the Siren, helped me understand it as a sign of deep psychosis and tragic unwellness.

Every day I woke up not only in a BFM but with what the Siren said it meant. Getting up, then, each day was a grief and an agony and a humiliation. But I also had some ability to know the things in my head were not as real as getting up. The things in my head were not as real as putting pants on and meeting people somewhere. The things in my head were not as real as being a person in a place.

This is what I'm thinking and feeling.

But it is not what I understand.

But it is not where I'm headed.

I'm headed toward putting on pants and walking out the door.

I realized that, though I felt awful and scared and awful, there was something in me that could get up anyway, that knew how to get up anyway. There was something more real and wild and close than the thoughts and the feelings. There was something that made it possible to get up anyway, and that was the trust I had in Christ. It was done with the trust I had in Christ.

I would get to the coffee shop sometimes in awe and wonder.

How did I get here?

I was dragged here by the trust I had in Christ. I was dragged into this small coffee shop by Christ's death and resurrection. By Word and Spirit. By understanding and intention.

I had to get used to the fact that this was the victory: getting up. Christ's death and resurrection wasn't feeling better or feeling worse. It was understanding and intention. It was knowing someone and heading somewhere.

I would get to the coffee shop right as it opened, order coffee just to have something to hold in my hand and put in my body. There was something healing, simple, and validating in being spoken to and given a cup of coffee. A few friends would arrive, order coffee, sit with me, and we would continue on in that long, ancient tradition of reading Scripture with people we love and praying about what happens to them. We did Morning Prayer, said the things you say, read the Psalms. And I don't have much of a reason to know why I did it, and kept doing it, and kept doing it, other than that getting up to hear Scripture and be led in prayer was what my life was now. And I did this, again and again and again and again, not because I enjoyed it so much, or because it made my life better, but because, somehow, in a way I didn't really have to think much about, I knew: "This is what life is. Life is like this now. This is what life is now."

My symptoms fluctuated. But that understanding deepened: this is what my life is now. There are millions of things that feel wrong, a million things to figure out, but only a few things I'm supposed to be doing. And this is one of them.

THE DIOCESE THAT DIDN'T WANT to ordain me was fine with letting me work for a mission agency that was more comfortable with my mental illness. It was a part-time job getting to know people on the street and keeping them company. Often I was happy, interested. But just as often I was tired, grumpy, struggling with the idea of myself as someone who rode around on a bike I borrowed from my wife, meeting and listening to beautiful, ugly, broken-down people like myself.

Still living with the soul's dissatisfaction.

I often stopped and thought to myself, "At one point, I had a career. I'd almost been given a church to pastor. And now, with this broken-down bike and part-time job, I have begun my life as a f—— nobody."

I would bob and weave down the roads, dodging traffic, eating at soup kitchens. I made friends with folks at a care home. One of them was a particularly close friend. We did Evening Prayer together. We would sit out on a stoop. He led and I listened, and when I listened life was no longer all the busy things in my head but the temperature outside and the sound of his voice and his reading of Scripture. I could let that cadence slow down my heart, my mind, let his deep voice set Life as I Would Have It before the Lord.

His voice helped me understand.

I knew, at times like that, I had a life in Christ that included me seeing him, and him seeing me. And something of my life in Christ would be immeasurably lost if I were to ever lose the way he read Scripture to me. The way he read Scripture turned my face toward Christ. The way he read Scripture was Christ's face turned toward me.

It would always be like this: my favorite way to be with Christ was to hear. My favorite way to hear was to close my eyes and to put my head down on a hard surface. And to become, somehow, that patient, quiet understanding. To become, despite everything, that hard kernel of patient, quiet trust. When I do it, it looks like I'm giving up, but what I'm trying to do is just become someone who hears.

Soon others joined us. The first was a young woman who wore a large hoodie and carried all her personal stuff in a backpack so no one would take her books or gel pens. At first while she listened, she stared at the floor, hoodie drawn tight across her face by the strings, too shy it seemed to even read out loud, and then one day, out of nowhere, she sang Psalm 27. Her voice was thin, high, persistent. Like a determined whisper.

I knew then, her reverence, her intention, was a sacrament. Tone and voice and timing just as much a sacrament as the blood and the wine because they held her complete trust in Christ. A torn Bible and her trembling sincerity was Christ's appearance in a place. It was the fact of Christ in a place.

THOSE BEAUTIFUL MOMENTS WERE HARD to convey. It was hard to tell people what I did for a living. Often hard to see any honor or glory in it, especially when friends of mine were getting ordained. And I was just a guy on a bike, sitting on a stoop, eating at soup kitchens. I wanted, deeply, to stop being a nobody. I wanted, deeply, the world to turn its face toward me again.

I remember walking with someone I met. He was in his forties. He walked with big floppy boots, and he liked cocaine and did construction. He maybe looked a little rough, but he was just one of the people I'd met walking and riding around.

He was walking with me, talking, looking back on his relationship to drugs, himself, and the Lord. We were both, I think, wishing we felt better about where we were at and what we were doing.

By that time it was Covid season and I couldn't see my friends at the care home. But during Covid, at 4:30, no matter what, I stopped what I was doing to do Evening Prayer with them over the phone.

I asked my friend I was walking with, who looked a little rough, and who I really didn't know that well, and who I was worried was a little too cool to be doing what I was about to ask him to do, if he would just stand here on the sidewalk and listen with me.

He nodded and then there we were, on a sidewalk downtown, two men just listening, to a voice coming through in fits and starts. We stood still as a man in a care home announced the gospel of Jesus Christ to us on speakerphone. The wind blew, we leaned in. We got as close as we could to just listening.

He read, "Why are you troubled, and why do doubts arise in your hearts?"

Scripture came through the speakers in fits and starts. The wind tore off syllables.

He read, "See my hands and my feet, that it is I myself. Touch me, and see."

We cannot return through effort or sorrow.

It is hearing that establishes us as a relation to Christ.

And, briefly, on that street, hearing was beholding.

Beholding the Christ who died.

The Scriptures want to reveal who Christ is. The written word wants to reveal the Eternal Word.

There He was. I had him by hearing.

The clothing of my shame.

The casting out of my fear.

The bearing of my history.

The enduring of My Affliction.

The overturning of my accusation.

The forgiveness of my sin.

Provision for my soul's unbearable dissatisfaction.

I would be changed by who He is. And changed into who I am. Servant and guest.

I picked up the Thread again.

I learned at coffee shops and care homes and on speaker phones, and was learning again, that a life in Christ is not cerebral; it is audible. That it comes to us, into us, through the mouths of folks we know. It wouldn't exist without someone to speak it to me. Because the gospel, especially when it is spoken out loud from the mouth of someone who isn't us, continues to have a power over our hearts we do not have. The very strength of a Christian's life, its very foundation, the very fact and basis of it, is its being announced by someone else.

Hearing is the place where Christ finds us. The only trust we have is the one that has been rescued by hearing. The hearing of the Word is the rescue of the human heart.

I saw myself then. The Howling Boy. A nobody, on his wife's bike.

We want so desperately to change so the world will turn its face toward us again. But the Lord operates differently. The Lord turns His face toward us that we might be changed. We are changed as we are seen by Christ.

"Why do doubts arise in your hearts? See my hands and my feet, that it is I myself."

"Why do doubts arise in your hearts? See my hands and my feet, that it is I myself."

I thought the problems in my life were things not lining up, things not working, the Lord not being clear, and that the people I worked with were stubborn and impossible. But here I had the gospel overruling the verdicts I'd made over myself and others.

And the problem was that I didn't have a heart the Lord could work with. The work was difficult. I would always be disfigured by the week at hand. And each week the gospel would have to create the heart that offers.

I cannot even overturn the hardness of my own heart.

The wounded hands. The forgiveness of Sin. The only place where mine becomes His.

You begin to realize, in the midst of all the pain and confusion and dissatisfaction of your life as a traumatized nobody with a mental illness, there would always be a John Who Trusts Christ, not because I can create him but because he is the creation of the Word of Mercy.

PEOPLE ASK YOU HOW YOU get better. And I said it before. The gift of humility, moments of reverence like this, were how I got better. If I have been given humility, I have been given a way back to myself. Humility, reverence is the condition of being pushed out of the center of your own life, like we are at funerals or when the stars come out. Humility and reverence is the condition of being pushed out of the center of your own life by the revelation of Who Christ Is. When Christ tells us who He is, He tells us who we are. It's how you learn your smallness without hating yourself. I've done, I've learned, more with my smallness than with anything else. And I've learned the holiest thing I have is my smallness.

The hearing of the gospel is the gift of humility. And the endurance of History and Affliction. How we bear What's Wrong and What Happened.

Only the gospel can reveal Christ to us. And because only the gospel can reveal Christ to us, only the gospel can reveal us to ourselves. Hidden within the proclamation of the gospel is who we are. Something about us—our true name as servants and guests—is always going to be hidden within our hearing of the gospel.

I lived as I sat down with these people on the street, as we approached His throne with coffee, and as I was vigilantly repositioned by Word and Spirit into something other than what I thought I was—not a terrifying god or worthless crazy piece of shit but something smaller, a goofy sojourner with a brain that worked in fits and starts, more fragile than I'd thought, vulnerable and somehow loved by God, a free man and not even knowing it. The gospel was continually setting me aside from ugly, bullying thoughts toward simple things, simple devotion, simple hearing, simple tasks. Better burdens. And I would go on from there, from Morning Prayer or Evening Prayer, and simply try to do one or two things well. I would try to pay attention to someone; I would try to go on a walk. I would try to work on a project. The Daily Office had a way of making my life about the few things I could do instead of everything I should.

At the end of the Daily Office, even if it was distracted, half-hearted, I would still feel that my day had become about something else. That it had changed around what I understood. That

I had somehow taken up the Thread. Being led through What Could Happen and What Should Happen along the narrow Thread of my intentions.

Hear, pray, offer.

Hear, pray, offer.

Hear, pray, offer.

It took me a long time, but I was really beginning to understand the Lord wasn't disappointed in me for having a mental illness. That my life in Christ was not given to me or taken from me by the wrong thoughts and the wrong feelings. And to get down to the ordinary business of becoming someone who depends on Christ. It was, and continues to be, the work of my life.

I was bound by a fearful, trembling body and a mind that worked in fits and starts. Making my way through wolves and rats no one could see and I could not get rid of. There was a lot, it seemed, I could not do. But I could wake up. I could put on pants. I could go out and meet people. I could read my Bible patiently, thoughtfully. And I could return to a Word that was not bound. I could be led by His Spirit. I could offer myself to His fellowship. I was determined, in this small way, that my ordinary life would be set aside by death of Christ and not by obsessive-compulsive disorder. I had to follow this Thread, understand that there was something to trust in other than my terrorized body, screaming brain, and soul in despair.

A life in Christ had always felt before like it was just inside me, that the life in Christ was as good as what my insides could do with it, a spontaneous combustion of virtue, insight, and affection within my own heart. But for months after the psych ward my life in Christ was something that had to be announced and handed to me, that had to be put in my hands, or stuffed in my ears. My life in Christ had to be a hand that led me gently away from destruction.

It had to shake me when my ex-missionary friend put his hand on my shoulder, to physically shake me when I was standing in the sun, when he could tell I was sad just by the way I mowed my lawn and pulled his goofy bicycle over—the one with the handlebar basket and clown horn—put his big hand on my shoulder, shook me back and forth, and let Words of Mercy fall from his lips and onto my head as I looked down and cried.

Seen, safe, fed. Anointed.

It took time, but I began to understand what an ordinary life in Christ is like. Extraordinary weeks of doing became ordinary weeks of learning to hear, learning to pray, learning to offer. And small, so small and intentional and slow.

Moment by moment, moment by moment.

Through the Wilderness of History and Affliction.

Through What's Wrong and What Happened.

And the way they live in us.

Following the way of the cross.

No one really wants to admit how small a life in Christ is. How it makes your life smaller so that it is bearable, how you're given something so precious—His Word, His Spirit, and with it something so small and ordinary—hearing and prayer, with tattered Bibles and the half-hearted movements of our mouths at coffee shops and care home steps. That that quiet Rhythm is precisely how Christ wants to make a life with us. That isn't just a dry routine. It is a rescue, a leading, a fulfillment of something. Of the trust we have in Christ. Trusting in Christ by hearing, trusting Christ with things through prayer. Learning to become quiet. Learning to become simple.

This life is one of great shame and fear and pride—forces that cannot be overcome by us. This Rhythm is precisely how Christ wants to bear this life with us, bear it for us. Precisely how He wants to unite our ordinary life to those extraordinary events. Precisely how He wants to overturn the shame and fear and pride with us, in us, for us. As we become quiet. As we become simple.

I could not get over how such extraordinary things are pledged to us in such ordinary ways. I could not get over the fact that, with so much danger inside and outside us, we are still asked to pay attention to something so small. A seed, a Word. The Scriptures. The sound of a raspy, halting voice bearing the Word to us. And to bear the fruit of that Word with great patience and care. To attend to it as it tends to us. To bear it patiently. And to do it with our own smallness. And to let it bury our hardness of heart, clothe our shame, cast out our fear. To let it be our share in His victory over sin and death.

And I was so small and distracted. So distracted and small. To be so small and distracted. To become quiet and simple, simple and quiet. Simple and quiet.

OFTEN WHEN WE DID MORNING Prayer or Evening Prayer there was so much distraction. So many voices inside and outside my head. The sound of people talking mixing with my own worries. Their rats and mine. Their wolves and mine.

When Covid-19 protocols lifted, and we could do Evening Prayer together at the care home, we did it in the cafeteria. The TV was on and it was blaring. And the sound coming from the TV was always the always booming, almost thoughtful voice of Dr. Phil. And if Dr. Phil's voice was not there, there was still the low murmur of other residents playing Uno, the unchecked rudeness of the staff, and the smell of someone else's urine.

Paying attention was something that simply was not possible.

Hearing was not possible.

Prayer was not possible.

We were huddled together, doing the best we could.

We could not pay attention. We could only head toward paying attention. We could only head toward hearing. We could only head toward prayer.

It was not possible to hear. And yet, hearing was the intention to hear.

It was not possible to pray. And yet, I knew, prayer was the intention to pray.

And I knew I had Christ not by thought or by feeling or by ability, but by understanding and intention. And Christ could create and rescue and lead our intentions. So that we could always head somewhere with Him.

There were days when my head and the world were so frantic. When all I had was the narrow Thread of my own shaking voice, reading Scripture out loud in a strange place. But the Thread, I learned, was still there. There to take hold, there to follow. Even if all you have is the narrow Thread of your own shaking voice. The narrow thread of your intentions. Even if all you have is the direction of the heart.

Word and understanding.

Spirit and intention.

I REMEMBER THE WEEK I HAD a Zoom meeting with my bishop, the chance, I thought, to explain myself, to show how much progress I'd made in not having a mental illness. I crafted all my arguments in my head ahead of time. I thought of every reason why what I wanted should be what happens.

I waited on the Zoom call for fifteen minutes. One of us had the wrong day, the wrong time. Nothing but silence. And I listened to that silence because it was kind and wise and when it was that quiet I felt a bit silly for how much fuss I made. It is the kind of quiet where the Lord lets us return to Him almost without us realizing it. Returning to Him, and to John who was a lot quieter, a lot smaller.

Neither god.

Nor Stranger.

In returning to Christ, I had been returned to the John Who Had Been Offered Mercy.

Neither god.

Nor Stranger.

But servant.

And guest.

In that moment, in that quiet, I saw my life as the small intake of breath between Christ is risen and Christ will come again. In light of Him dying and Him coming again, many things simply do not matter as much. Other things, like kissing my wife and sitting down and listening to someone, mattered more.

The world changed around what I understood.

I was reminded of letters I hadn't sent to people who could really use a letter.

I was reminded of books I'd been making, prayer books I made out of computer paper, foam board, and placemats, the streamlined Daily Office booklets I made for people I work with on the street. The only way to do a decent job making them is to measure carefully. To become as small as measuring foam boards carefully.

I was reminded I could depend on Christ by making books and writing letters. And by being quiet.

There, cutting foam boards, using a needle and thread to make a bound book, and talking to Jesus while I do it, I am no longer conformed to passions of my former ignorance. I am holy. I could lie on the floor and be the Lord's small thing.

I could do it, I could become this painfully simple.

Anxiety would be no defense against this, against my smallness, against this Pentecost of small obediences.

I thought holiness at first was things made shiny. But it seems like it's old things, odd things, like drawing or typing something, buying toothpaste for my wife, or visiting someone.

We cannot see trust, but it consecrates everything we can see.

Every ordinary thing set aside by hearing and prayer, Word and Spirit, death and resurrection.

Holiness was ordinary things set aside for God by trust in Him, a holy life was an ordinary life with ordinary things that have been offered to Christ. Only Christ could make a life holy, and out of His sheer Mercy He would make an ordinary life holy, make it His, through Word and Spirit, Scriptures that could be heard, and prayers that could be spoken, offerings made with trembling bodies. Trusting in Christ, trusting Christ with things. Simple things that could be done again and again. And what was the great holiness in this? What was the great wisdom in that kind of life?

That when we cannot think, we can hear.

When we cannot feel, we can speak.

When we cannot imagine a future, we can look down and see we are still making books. We are still writing letters. The Thread is still there. We are going to be okay.

And I wrote in my journal, "I have a bike, I have time, and a gospel that was stuffed in my ears until it broke open my heart. I have, vividly and powerfully, the Memory of that heart breaking when that Word was spoken. And when I pedal, I pedal with an anointing and sacred calm of that News: Christ has died, Christ is risen, Christ will come again."

Servant.

Guest.

Servant.

Guest.

I am bound by a mental illness, a small bike, and a part-time salary. But it is a mental illness, a small bike, and a part-time job that can be offered to Christ. And in that way, such silly things are sacraments. And this ordinary life I have, and you have, can be offered to Christ and become sacred that way. Not extraordinary but sacred. I can begin to take joy in the difference.

Everything that has made my life beautiful has also made it small.

A big man, a small bike, a part-time salary. All three things are Christ's and all three things, I hope, consecrated.

The gospel did not reveal itself to scrutiny, to careful searching. It was not revealed to geniuses or to scholars, scientists drawing elaborate equations. It was revealed to the poor and to idiots like me. Who pedal on a bike smiling when there doesn't seem to be a reason to, smiling anyway, smiling with a secret that is no secret: Christ has died, Christ is risen, Christ will come again."

CHRIST IS RISEN

In the Wilderness of History and Affliction

PART III
THE SWIMMING

THERE WAS SOMETHING ELSE I did every day. Or almost every day.

I went swimming.

I would get up before Morning Prayer and go swimming. I didn't want to but I did. When I got into my trunks and onto the edge of the pool, I rubbed tired eyes. And waited. And waited. Until my unwilling limbs were thrown into the water by the trust I had in Christ. With a leap into cold water I was released from the Realm of Ceaseless Cognition and delivered into the fact of my big shivering body.

Other people swam laps, limbs carving up the water. I swam under the water like a torpedo or a slow fish. Being under the water felt like flying.

When my goggles broke, I swam with eyes closed, put my hand on the bottom of the pool, on the length of blue tile that ran from one end of the pool to the other. It had a different texture than the bottom of the pool that was otherwise white and bumpy. I would dive down, scrape my chest on the bumpy stuff, and reach out for the tile. I would swim at the bottom of the pool, my hand dragging on the tile, eyes closed, the skin on the tip of my fingers nicked and calloused by the upturned tile edges. And I knew, if I found the long blue tile, I would get to the other end of the pool without having to look or think.

In the pool I was gifted with visions. They were understandings in my heart. As I dragged my hand along the tile I understood in my heart that my mind was a long hallway, with doors on either side, going all the way to the end.

Each door in that hallway was a way that I consoled myself, a kind of thinking I got myself into, a door into the Realm of Ceaseless Cognition. Inside each door I walked through I would either plead my case so I would be okay, condemn someone so I would be okay, or figure something out so that I would be okay. Each door was a place where Life as I Would Have It could be fixed, obtained, negotiated, managed. Each door was a place where I could make things right.

But when I swam, I knew in my heart I was not in the Realm of Ceaseless Cognition. I was not in that grand, haunting, teeming, complicated place. I was in a long hallway.

At the end of this long pool lane with the tile I dragged my hand along, there was a cross made of those same blue tiles. When I arrived at the blue cross at the end of pool, I understood at the end of the hallway Jesus was dying on His big dumb cross.

When I was holding my breath and dragging my hand on that tile and looking at the cross at the end of the pool, I knew there was a very specific location of Reality. It was the exact spot where the Son of God died. To look down that hallway, to look down the end of the pool, was to know Reality was not some vague horizon, but a cross, a single transcendent point of attention outside of how you think and feel. Because the cross is not interested, ultimately, in what we think or how we feel. It is interested in what things are.

And this is important because when your mind is not you, and when your mind is not your friend at all, and when your mind is a vivid, compelling, and brutal son of a bitch, and when all it does is lie to you and keep your body in terror and grieve you terribly and keep your soul in despair, then what you want most at that point is not to feel better or to feel worse but to be judged, handed over, delivered by Reality.

You want to know what's true. You want to be changed by who He is.

Reality, I learned (and was learning), was not a given. Delusion was a given. Insanity was a given. Reality was gift, rescue, and intervention. Reality would always be outside me, because it would always be the cross of Christ and not me. It would always be the Mercy that was offered. And I would always be the understanding that Mercy had been offered, its servant and guest. It would always have Reality, more than I could ever understand. And I would have this patient, quiet understanding. And those few simple intentions.

And the Word of the cross at the end of the hallway, and the way of the cross along this blue tile, was the only thing that could be called sight and not blindness.

A cross. Driven into the ground two thousand years ago. What a small and pitiful and peculiar and desperate thing to hang a life on, and yet it had borne the weight of my whole life.

Placing my hand on that tile, I realized that through the relentless, diligent repetition of this Rhythm it had begun to become, finally, a choice to go to the cross, to go down the hallway and not through the door. I had other things I could do, other ways I could live. Through an Ordinary Life of Regular Worship, it was no longer inevitable that I would end up in the Realm of Ceaseless Cognition.

THE RHYTHM MAYBE TAUGHT ME nothing new, but it had deepened my trust in what I already knew. And with that deepened trust, I could trust Christ with what I had not expected. Having begun to hear, I could begin to pray.

Earlier in my recovery, I had already trusted Christ with what I had not expected.

I remember when I was first out of the psych ward, being so ashamed of those intrusive thoughts and praying they would go away. But one day, while praying, I felt in my heart that Christ could be shown these thoughts without harm to him or me. I felt he'd seen it already, felt it already. That everything we could be made to see and feel had been seen and felt by Christ.

And so I showed him things. I pretended, in my head, I was taking Christ on a tour of my worst intrusive thoughts. The thoughts whose presence I thought was intolerable. I showed him the things I was afraid to show anybody, and I made this tour a prayer to Christ. Those intrusive thoughts hung like paintings or sat like statues, leaping out ineffectively. The idea of praying so that they would go away was not new; the idea of bringing the thoughts I could not get rid of into my life of prayer was very new.

I didn't realize those thoughts could occupy the same space as that patient, quiet understanding. That worst of my intrusive thoughts could become a time of patient waiting on the Mercy offered in the gospel.

How come? How could those intrusive thoughts occupy the same space as that patient, quiet understanding? Because of who He is. Because Jesus makes the unclean clean.

That had been a breakthrough.

But I was going to have to trust Christ with something else.

In that hallway, without a door to go through, I began to feel an agonizing, squeezing heartache. It was hard to say what it was. I was free, finally, to not engage in my compulsion. I could swim past the Siren. But I also felt, in that hallway, so compromised, and so terrifyingly vulnerable. I felt all the humiliation brought on by the onset and aggravation of my mental illness. The full brunt of that unbearable dissatisfaction. The deep rupture it had been in my life. The sudden revolt and despair. The pain of how I had been treated, the deep sadness and anger over what my life was like now.

I did not know what to do with what I was feeling if there was no door I could go into to make it better. I began to wonder, again, if there was anything worse than feeling this way.

I realized again where compulsions come from: if there is something we want to do, something we want to figure out, something we want to make right, something we want to know for sure, there is usually something we don't want to feel.

An uncertainty we cannot bear.

A tension we cannot stand.

A confusion we cannot abide.

A temptation we cannot live with.

A pain we cannot tolerate.

I swam up to the cross-shaped tile at the end of the pool. I went under water and pressed my submerged head against it. I brought the things I hated about myself, the surprising and unnameable grief, all that deep, blinding pain into a fist that I hurtled through water and hit the cross-shaped tile with. I could close my eyes and see myself in that hallway, slamming my fists on that cross and cursing, howling. My mind unraveled, and I said all of the most hurtful and horrible and unmentionable things into the wood and nailed feet. I said all the things I will not say here.

Then I dove to the bottom of the pool, spinning like a slow whale, talking to Jesus the whole time, letting myself be angry or weird, letting myself be very upset, letting myself be frightened of myself, as long as it was in front of Christ, as long as I knew Christ was there for all of it. As long as I could trust Christ with it. It is hard to tell somebody what this is like, but it is somehow like finally realizing you've been holding something all to yourself, and that your holding it to yourself has been and is the problem and you didn't even know it. That you've been this blind and didn't even know it.

That there is something worse than the experience of shame and fear. And it is our addiction to handling it ourselves.

And offering that shame and fear and unbearable dissatisfaction to Christ by yelling through chlorinated water.

I needed a way to be very upset.

That was what reverence was. A way to be very upset.

Jesus is the only way I get over things.

I would tell people banging on that tile with an underwater fist was like a sweet, agonizing, piercing wound opening up, and with it, this understanding in my heart:

Nearer than what can be seen and felt. A trust as deep as the wound.

And after, the quiet in the pool all around me. Limbs floating. A heart kept in the stillness at the cross. That patient, quiet understanding, carved deeper than I could have ever hoped or wanted.

The reason so few of us grow in our life in Christ is because it is so painful. There is no growth to our dependence on Christ that is not also a wound to our dependence on self.

We do not often realize how deep the shame, the fear, the discouragement goes. Our shame, fear, and discouragement are so deeply attached to our way of dealing with it, of managing it, that we are not able to distinguish them. Our shame and fear have made us so vulnerable to our dependence on ourselves. A dependence on ourselves that is so deep we cannot see or feel or find or know about it.

We are not able to separate our pain from the way we've dealt with it. Unable to separate pain and consolation. Unable to separate the fact of pain and humiliation from the way we have understood and handled it.

I realized, again, there were two Johns. There was the John I met in my intrusive thoughts, a John bizarre, impossible, and condemned. He was not a John that I could fix, or understand, or defend. I still don't know where he comes from. But I've realized he doesn't matter very much. He is simply a bizarre, uninterpretable hieroglyphic.

But there was another John, the John who was ashamed, afraid, and discouraged by those thoughts. The Howling Boy who'd had to suffer them, that had to bear them. The Howling Boy in the grip of the mind's intimidation and the body's anticipation. And he mattered very much. Because he was the one who'd done the Suffering.

And it was the Howling Boy who was with me in that long hallway called prayer.

The one who had to live with What's Wrong and What Happened.

It was not the John I saw in my intrusive thoughts who was being addressed by God. It was the Howling Boy who was ashamed, afraid, and discouraged by them, who felt hopeless and anguished, distressed, and in despair by this life and by this illness and by What Happened. The Howling Boy was the John who was being addressed, who was being led in that long hallway. And he was the John I would have to stay with. The one who would have to be led to the cross.

The Howling Boy was alone in a great long hallway called prayer. I'd found him. Or, now, he'd found me.

I'd met him before, here and there. But here I bear the full brunt of him. The full brunt of what he could make me feel.

The symptoms of my OCD had cleared up enough for me to meet him again.

And it was just him and Jesus and this great and terrible feeling: that the world had turned its face from me, that the world was not safe, that too much had been taken. That life was unbearable and I was alone.

I didn't know what to do. And so I began to yell at God again, to scream in the water, and to hit the cross-shaped tile.

I would wonder, later, how I got to yell at God like that, to get away with being that way. Getting away with being, dare I say it? Unstable? Not put together? Not happy? Very upset? How do I get to be like that?

The Siren was afraid of the Howling Boy. And told me he was unacceptable, that his deep, anguished grief was unacceptable. Loathsome. That something was deeply, horribly wrong with him.

Perhaps me and the Siren were in agreement. I was afraid of him too. Reluctant. Repulsed.

But the Lord is not afraid of us like we are of ourselves. That is His Mercy. He is not afraid of us like we are of ourselves.

And to hit the cross that way, and to hit and smash it often, is to know that our anger, our unbearable dissatisfaction, can't hurt God the way it can hurt other people. That our anger, our unnameable grief, belongs at the throne with the wounded Son, the only place where our anger is holy.

With that anger, with that outburst, the Lord had got so close that I could honestly say, with that sweet, piercing, heartache, the humiliation was shared. The humiliation was ours.

If our screaming and our howling have been consecrated, then our screaming and howling is the fear of the Lord. It is the trust we have in Christ. It is trusting Christ with things. We think Christ is honored by what we think and feel. But Christ is honored by what we trust him with.

What had I done in the swimming pool? What had I done with an Ordinary Life of Regular Worship?

I had trusted Christ with what had been taken.

It had been consecrated. It had become His. Word and Spirit had been joined to my humiliation the way it had joined the bread and the wine and the waters of baptism. That unbearable dissatisfaction had been made holy by its proximity to Christ. Everything that could be seen and felt or done or taken was now the blood poured out and the body broken for us. Everything that could be seen, felt, done, or taken had been given back to us as Himself, as the forgiveness of sins.

Worship is the process of making ugly things available to Christ. It is the removal of those things that have kept our pain hidden from us. All those ugly, horrible, beautiful, powerful things we can't even begin to name but that flood us suddenly, inexplicably. A Christian is someone whose pain must become terrifyingly available to Christ, so that our pain and all its humiliations do not take on their own secret life as an object of worship.

Perhaps that is what it means to live simply and quietly with Christ. We must make those things that most pain and frighten us available to Christ, and especially those things that pain and frighten us most. We must bring him what we've been made to see and feel, must bring him what's been taken, must bring it before all the tenderness and severity of Christ. And especially as we find them in those things that pain and frighten us most: prior versions of ourselves. The one made to bear the Affliction. The one who bore the brunt of History. The Howling Boy we are still are.

I BOUGHT AN ICON OF THE raising of Lazarus that hangs over the desk where I write. In the icon, Christ is sovereign and unconcerned, but Lazarus is not. Lazarus is confused. He has been given a resurrection, and it has not erased confusion. He has been redeemed by God, but he has no story. He is still wrapped in the bandages of the tomb. He is still scared. What is so powerful and frightening to me about this resurrection is its severity. Perhaps His death is our consolation; it is His resurrection that must make us tremble.

I do not know what first drew me to this icon. Perhaps it said what I did not know how to say. I do not know how to best articulate this, but it was always the resurrection that filled me with such confusion and frustration and dread. Perhaps it is the resurrection that I've never understood, the way Christ, after having regarded us so profoundly at the cross, now turns His face away and says, "Come after me." And takes us where we do not want to go.

Perhaps it was best to say it this way. I was consoled to know the risen Christ was still crucified. That even in heaven He remains the Christ Who Died. And I was terrified to know the crucified Christ was risen. Because it meant we had to follow Him. We had to be dragged by the Spirit. We had to be dragged by the trust we had in Him.

It is a frightening thing to be reborn, to be reborn and to be led, hobbling, to what things are, to be led. To stand there with all the pain, doubt, confusion, and intolerable dissatisfaction and for this to be called hope. To be led by hope through the intolerable, the unimaginable, the unintelligible. To learn that hope is not a feeling and not even the end of despair but the leading of the trust that had been rescued through hearing.

What I take it to mean is that confusion and disorientation and pain and pilgrimage are part of the resurrection, not outside of it.

I knew it when I walked through a cemetery on Easter Sunday with a man I was learning was my friend.

We talked back and forth about little things. Then we looked at the graves.

Christ's resurrection, my friend said, doesn't mean the graves are empty. And the resurrection, since it is not, yet, our health being healed, our jobs being kept, or hearts swept perfectly clean, is always leading us. And because we have His resurrection and still die, and because we have His resurrection and still mourn, and because we have His resurrection and still do not have answers, and because we have His resurrection and still have intrusive thoughts and perilous feelings, then His resurrection is a leading and not an arrival. His resurrection is our pilgrimage. And to have the risen Christ is for your life to become a Wilderness of miraculous provision.

THE TRUST THAT HAD BEEN rescued through hearing was then led in prayer. And led where I did not want to go.

I stepped out of the Realm of Ceaseless Cognition into a frightening emotional landscape. And I began to call it prayer.

When Christ rescued the Howling Boy from the Realm of Ceaseless Cognition, I followed Christ—limping, crying, and screaming—into the great Wilderness of prayer.

I was able, painfully, to not fall into excessive rumination. Or to at least catch myself when I did.

But without that means of consolation suddenly, out of nowhere, and in my day-to-day life, the present tense became full of anger, anguish, boredom, irritation, and deep confusion. I bore the full brunt of the mind's screaming, the body's peril, and the soul's despair. Everything got harder. To be there, to be in the unadorned present tense without my compulsions, was something that could only be done with, still to this day, real discomfort and at times incredible pain.

It is such a naked and vulnerable thing to walk into the great Wilderness of what you are feeling with only the trust you have in Christ and its prosaic, half-hearted expressions in prayer. The painful simplicity of prayer. To be rescued from the power of sin is to be released into the pain, confusion, and dissatisfaction of your actual life.

And how to bear it? How to bear the sudden irritation, the dark mood, the anger, the confusion? When you can't go into your head and make it better? When your mind isn't getting what it wants? When you have to wait there like a toothache. With nothing to console your confusion.

I thought, again, of the disciples on the boat in the storm.

What were the disciples supposed to do? They had already heard Christ's call to turn and follow. They weren't supposed to return to Christ through hearing, they had already been called, they were already with him. They already had His Word.

They were supposed to feel that peril, that sensation of drowning, that heaving grief and learn to wait. They were supposed to stand there and wait on Christ. And wait there with Christ. In the sinking boat.

And this could be done in prayer. Prayer is how we wait on the Lord. Prayer is how I drowned and how I learned I would not drown. How I learned even shame, fear, and despair could be the deepening of my trust in Christ.

There was a very specific way I learned to pray, to make my way through the present tense. I did it with a very, very, old prayer from the Eastern Orthodox tradition. The Jesus Prayer.

I breathed in and prayed, "Lord, Jesus Christ." I breathed out and prayed, "Have Mercy on Me, a sinner." I learned to do it all the time.

The Jesus Prayer was something I would do in a car. Sometimes I would put my head against the AC, turn the air all the way up, until my life was as simple as the air in my face and how I was feeling and what I was saying to Jesus Christ.

Over the years and with that prayer, I learned every beautiful, dull, and horrible feeling—whether from body, mind, or soul—could be borne patiently and with Christ.

It didn't make the things go away, the pull of the OCD. It didn't stop the storm, stop the undertow of the Siren; it didn't end my desire to know for sure, my desire to figure things out. It didn't end the soul's unbearable dissatisfaction.

It did not immediately console the Body That Expected the World to End.

It didn't make powerful feelings go away, but it revealed to me a feeling was a feeling. And that was all it was. Prayer was how I learned that I could not be destroyed by what I was feeling (whether from body, mind, or soul) and that an ordinary life was possible with a mind that screamed, a body that cringed, a soul that howled. Something understood with great, painful simplicity.

Prayer was the place where the omens and the prophetic utterances of the Siren and the Body That Expected the Word to End were revealed moment by moment to be untrue. It was where I could stand with the Howling Boy. I could experience all of it and still live. I could live, painfully, moment by moment with Christ.

Lord Jesus Christ, have Mercy on me.

Lord Jesus Christ, have Mercy on me.

Lord Jesus Christ, have Mercy on me.

On one Fourth of July, fireworks erupted on all sides of my house. My wife wanted to go out and watch. This would have usually been an easy thing to say yes to. But today my brain felt horrible. It felt like if I went outside, I would die. I did go outside. But every moment standing next to her and having to watch fireworks was a cruelty and an agony.

Holding my wife's hand was a lesson in excruciating pain. The unadorned present tense, simply being present in my life, was a crucifixion.

The Siren said,

It was wrong.

It was intolerable.

And something bad would happen.

The Siren awoke a Body That Expected the World to End. My body cringed, and withdrew into itself.

My screaming mind and traumatized body awoke my soul's anguish. The despair at having to still live like this.

Didn't I used to enjoy fireworks?

Why was this so hard?

This would be a time, usually, to wonder why, to look for meaning, to use thoughts to feel better and figure out and to escape the moment I'm in. But instead I stood there and said the Jesus Prayer and accepted the fact that I felt horrible but that, also, serving my wife was more important than feeling better. I had barred the door to the Realm of Ceaseless Cognition. I would not, could not, go into my head to make it better, to make it right. There was nothing I could do to fix it. So I would stand there in prayer and not fix it.

And do it with the agonizing freedom of that patient, quiet understanding. I would stand there and love my wife and wait to be destroyed by what I could be made to feel.

And understand that I just had an Affliction. This Affliction and that understanding could occupy the same space.

That it was only that something had happened. And that What Happened now lived in my body.

I knew, standing in the yard, holding my wife's hand, that the secret intention of my life had been to feel better instead of feeling worse. To avoid and honor the Siren. To avoid the terror of a terrorized body. To run away from that unbearable dissatisfaction. I would do almost anything to not feel what I could be made to feel by body, mind, and soul. The incredible verdicts of shame, fear, and dread. The alarm bells and flare signals that could be rocketed toward me. The warnings and commands. The cringing. The howling.

But now there was nothing I could do but be there. Because, now I knew, there were things more important than feeling better, and feeling safe.

There was something more important than feeling okay.

I had, in Christ, the excruciating freedom to trust Christ and not fix it. I had, in Christ, the ability to withstand myself. To trust Christ with those Strangers by not trying to fix them. To stand with those Strangers and choose to feel bad. Simply. Painfully.

And it was there, with those fireworks, that I got to meet the thing itself, this thing that had caused so much trouble. The Siren that awoke the body's terror and the soul's despair.

It sat in the back of my head, and felt like a clawing, dying animal. Without the fog of cognition I could see it clearly: this little blinking light in my brain that said something was wrong when there was nothing wrong. The Siren that could pump all the wrong information into my brain, that said, "Dread! Confusion! Extreme Irritability!" when there was nothing but cool July evening and a beautiful sky. I could, with something close to serenity, inspect and observe what I was feeling without being pulled into it. I could feel the pull of it without being sucked in. I could make myself available to its intensity without honoring its interpretation. It created a feeling that had a droning, mechanical intensity. A dark, sucking pull.

Something is wrong.

Something is intolerable.

Something bad is about to happen.

But it was not taking me with it. I knew who was talking. I could be as involved with it as I wanted to be.

That clawing animal in my head, that blinking light, that air horn, was vivid, was powerful. But it was no god. It could be understood as an experience rather than worshiped as a deity.

Yes, I could have scary thoughts, and scary feelings, and not be scared and not be scary. It was only the thoughts and feelings we trust that get to kill us.

THE SIREN WAS A RELENTLESS and rushed turn toward dark and ominous meaning. Meanings that my terrorized body and despairing soul liked to believe. The Siren jumped to conclusions. But prayer, and specifically the Jesus Prayer, was a place where meaning was delayed. Delayed by way of patient, quiet trust.

Prayer was the crucial, agonizing, terrifying delay between how things feel and what things are. A place to wait and to endure experience without applying meaning. Prayer was the place where I gave myself time to not know for sure. A place where, though I felt all the intense power of the Siren, the pleading of my own body's peril, the brunt of my soul's despair, I did not defend, fix, or manage them.

It was where I listened to the Strangers that my body, mind, and soul had become. It was where I trusted Christ and listened to them but was not misshapen by their urgency.

Even as I suffered that kind of extreme discomfort, I learned beautiful, life-giving distinctions in prayer.

I learned something can be very powerful without being at all meaningful.

That a desire is not an intention.

I learned that uncertainty, tension, conflict, doubt, complication, tedium, transition, agitation, frustration, confusion, anger, and temptation are not intolerable and not even a sign that something is wrong but just a part of being human.

I learned that in prayer, Christ could be our

Peace in anger.

Simplicity in confusion.

Steadfastness in temptation.

Certainty in uncertainty.

Standing-place in intimidation.

Stillness in frustration.

You can go into a grocery store and experience an intrusive thought, you can sit down with a loved one and experience a horrible and overwhelming dread, you can be asked to help out with something and stand in awe and wonder at one's own horrifying irritation and mood, you can wake up deeply confused and horrible for no discernable reason, feel a dark and awful draw toward something, and in all of this not have surrendered in the least one's own faithfulness to Christ.

You have not sinned.

You have only experienced.

And you begin to learn, gradually, that those powerful experiences that may never dim in their intensity simply don't mean very much. You begin to understand what they are.

This may appear a bitter and strange victory. My life is still chock full of thoughts I don't like and feelings I don't trust (and also, with it: thoughts I don't trust, and feelings I don't like). But the miracle, as I count it, is what horrible things mean to me. Now a horrible feeling is no longer a reason to stop and think. I learned that just because my body is afraid doesn't mean that I am. That I could quietly meet my soul's dissatisfaction.

I became more and more bold, more and more able to go into places and try to do things. As long as I was willing to accept confusion and pain and dissatisfaction. To accept pain willingly by way of that patient, quiet understanding. To gently lead the Strangers that my body, mind, and soul had become.

To understand they could provide experiences but not verdicts. And to claim Mercy as the way forward. And to claim Mercy as the way forward for all of us.

Lord, have Mercy.

Lord, have Mercy.

Lord, have Mercy.

I would go into Costco and experience very intense fear, dread, confusion. And I could see that, although I was afraid, confused, and uncomfortable, that was all I was. I was not running to the blackboard of my mind. I was not fighting verdicts, and dodging accusations. I was not turning the wrong thoughts into right thoughts. I could stand with Christ and patiently endure the thing that said something was wrong when nothing was wrong.

I began to understand body, mind, and soul as a crying child. A child that might never grow up. The child I would have to live with.

It wailed and wailed, but I could tuck it close and keep going. Yes they could scream, yes they could yell, and yes they mattered, but they had to learn that we were going somewhere. Into my dependence on Christ. Into the future provided by Mercy.

They only needed gentle leadership of that patient, quiet understanding. They only needed to learn we were headed somewhere. Headed to Jesus, headed to Costco.

I would carry them the rest of my life. I could live with them; I could make peace with them. But I couldn't fix them. I only needed a way to live alongside what they were like now.

And that was okay.

The Siren cry, the cry of the Howling Boy, and the cry of a traumatized body were, often, similar. They hardly ever took turns speaking. They often piled in together.

It took years to distinguish them. Years of listening to them. Years of standing with them.

It was only over years being in that Rhythm that it slowly became possible to distinguish them, and give them names.

The Siren was an excruciating, piercing sensation in my head. Like a spider bite along the side of my head. Its shame, fear, and dread always felt dry and mechanical. It was the easiest to identify. It was always razors in my head. It felt more like a machine that wasn't working.

The Body That Expected the World to End was a dark jet of hot black fear in my chest. A squeezing tightrope feeling in my heart. It felt less mechanical, more primal, more organic. It felt like a living thing in my rib cage. Felt like something desperate curled up in my innards. It was the next easiest to find. It had a physical location. Its intensity had a geography, and could be mapped along my body. What Happened was in my breathing, in my chest.

The cry of the Howling Boy had a deeper undercurrent than both; it pulled from a deeper place. And it scared me more. It was a discouragement, a revolt. It was the hardest to find and name. My own soul's pain was the hardest to find and name. It was the hardest thing for me and Jesus to find and name.

And the more I was able to withstand the intimidation of the mind, the more I could attend to the anticipation of the body.

The more I could withstand the intimidation of the mind and attend to the anticipation of the body, the more I was able to stand with the soul in despair.

THE TRUTH WAS THAT MY pull into the darkness of OCD and trauma didn't happen in isolation. My slide into madness was concurrent with a relationship with an emotionally and spiritually abusive mentor. This relationship had gone on for over seven years. I wish to speak of it only briefly. The individual in question is no longer, as far as I know or wish to know, in ministry. But there was a terrible, awful thing he did to me. And what he did matched what the Siren did to me.

He slowly but surely created a world where only he could be trusted, and then he began to make me believe things that were not true. As his power over me grew, so did the Siren's. It was as though they had some inexplicable alliance, as though they met regularly in some dark room to discuss me. As if they both worked together, merged to become the Bully, and the Accuser.

After the traumatic visit to the psych ward, his treatment of me worsened. It was as if I was finally vulnerable enough for him to pounce on. There was as a day when his abuse became overt: psychological intimidation, emotional blackmail. He'd had a bad week. He was in obvious distress. And I finally saw who he was. I saw what he would do to be okay. I met the dark pull of what he would do to be okay.

I let the authorities in the diocese know and nothing really happened.

Perhaps if I had not just been in the psych ward I would have hung in there, gutted it out.

But, Mercy of Mercy, I knew I was too vulnerable to stay. Too vulnerable to depend on myself. With the help of a few close friends, I was able to leave him.

But when I left him, I also left the church I'd loved and the close friends I'd made in that church. And so, within the span of six months I lost

My mind.

My church.

My career.

And so, along with the trauma of the psych ward visit, I was forced to deal with all the pain and grief and trauma that go with emotional and spiritual abuse. And to reckon with its enmeshment with my OCD. The way it all piles in there together and the way only Jesus gets to sort it out.

The way it becomes something only Mercy could untangle:

The immense tangle of the Siren and the Howling Boy and the Body That Expected the World to End.

To lose only my mind or my church or my career would have been a deep grief. But I'd lost all of them. And when I found that grief, or rather, when it found me, it was a howl I didn't know I could bear.

When I left the Realm of Ceaseless Cognition, that grief was waiting in the Wilderness. There was no way around it. Facing it was part of resurrection life.

I had not got rid of being human. Life in His Spirit is not the avoidance of being human. It is being fully human before the face of Mercy.

The sudden availability of this grief, my sudden turn toward being available for it, my sudden desire to stand and turn and face my grief and anger and discouragement was more than I had bargained for, more than I knew how to talk about or deal with.

I simply didn't know it was possible to hurt this much. And I didn't know where these emotions would take me, how far down they would carry me. And that they could be such big, scary things.

And when the cry of my soul joined the cry of my mind and the cry of my body, their combined howl could be so alarming and dreadful.

One day I stood under a tarp during a thunderstorm, and when the wind howled, I thought of the howling of mind, soul, and body. I thought of the desires of my heart, this sudden irritation, my howling mood. My anger, my worry, my hurt. The pain of what had been said and what had been done. Why does everyone else, I thought, get to change their hearts and minds and feelings, when it seems I only get to withstand them?

Word and Spirit, gospel and Rhythm, death and resurrection, understanding and intention, was only a way of standing with all the pain, confusion, and dissatisfaction. And trusting Christ with it somehow.

I only had a place to stand with the pull of the Siren and the Howling Boy and the Body That Expected the World to End.

How could I be with these Strangers and make them friends again? How could I be available to them, care for them, without handing myself over to them, without forming an alliance with them? Shepherd them without being shepherded by them? How could I begin to understand that I was not the Siren's screaming or the body's terror or even my own soul's dissatisfaction? That I was the one keeping them company with that patient, quiet understanding?

All of them grabbed at me. All of them demanded consolation. All they wanted was to be okay. What they demanded was the consolation of story.

The Siren and the Howling Boy, in particular, wanted a story to make things right, to console them. They wanted a plan, an answer, a map. They wanted justice through narrative.

They wanted me to know for sure, make things right, defend them.

But I had no way to. I had no narrative.

I didn't have an answer to why people did things. I didn't have an explanation as to why things were what they were. I didn't know why I felt this way. I didn't know how to figure myself out, figure other things out. I didn't know how long I would be this way. I couldn't go into my head to make things better.

I did not have a story. I only had what I was feeling, what I could be made to see and feel by body, mind, and soul. All I had was the John Who Feels This Way. The John Who Feels This Way was all I had. And all I could do was not turn my face from him.

I did not have an understanding of this or that situation.

I did not have an understanding of this or that relationship.

I did not have an understanding of this or that person.

I did not have an understanding of this intrusive thought or perilous feeling.

All I had was

My frustration with this or that situation.

My hurt over this or that relationship.

My dread about this or that person.

My dread, shame, discomfort over this or that intrusive thought and perilous feeling.

But meaning was what I didn't have. And prayer was about giving myself time to not know what things meant. Prayer was the suspension of my heart and mind's relentless pleading for narrative. Its perilous drive toward meaning.

Meaning was something precious, something that would have to be gradually sorted out by hearing, through prayer, in offering. It would have to be sorted out gradually with Christ. Something gradually sorted out through Word and Spirit, hearing and prayer, patient understanding and diligent intention.

UNDER THAT TARP, THE WIND and rain picked up. Then there was a big gust of wind, and I felt everything shift but nothing move. The tarp had been tethered to the ground, and I could hold on to the metal spokes. And knew I had been given a small place to stand with Christ. A rope to hold on to. A place to stand against the thoughts of my mind and the cries of my heart. A place to stand when our thoughts and feelings scare us. A place to overcome by not being overcome. I had been given a small place to stand with Christ and withstand myself, and it was a place called prayer. I could stand with Christ and patiently bear the thing in my head that said something was wrong when nothing was wrong. I could stand with a trembling body. I could stand with Christ in that current of deep emotion, and deep pain and grief, and feel the brunt of it without it taking me away with it.

I was not as sturdy as the rope I'd been given. And I didn't need to be.

Lord Jesus Christ, have Mercy on me.

Lord Jesus Christ, have Mercy on me.

Lord Jesus Christ, have Mercy on me.

All I could be is with Christ. And it was all I needed to be.

I got better at standing there. Finding a place to stand and letting those experiences pass through. And learning they were not a problem to be solved but a Wilderness to be experienced. Strangers to show hospitality to.

Deeper than the pull of a mental illness, steadier than the pull of emotions, was the Christ I met in prayer, the Christ I yelled at in prayer. An anchor deeper, closer, surer than the stories we tell ourselves.

And our deepest, most painful emotions are often tied to the wrong stories. Stories that make us hate ourselves. Stories that make us hate others. Stories that leave us vulnerable to our dependence on ourselves.

There were days more awful than I want to remember. Days I would feel the deep lurch of grieving, the body's leaping terror, the Siren's hysterical screaming. But I would also understand I was okay. But I would also understand that I had been given a sound mind, a quiet mind to suffer with. And the word for this, I learned, was recovery.

Until then I did not know that grieving was different from thinking. That anger was different from thinking. That those emotions could be protected from Ceaseless Cognition. I did not know I could separate pain and interpretation. That I could sever how I felt from how I dealt with it. That in prayer, I could focus down until it was just me and Jesus and this big scary feeling.

And when I felt miserable, I would say, "I don't know what this is. I don't know what it is I'm feeling. I don't know what this is. But whatever it is, it is my life."

All I know is that I'm angry.

All I know is that I'm frustrated.

All I know is that I'm very upset.

All I know is that I'm very discouraged.

And all I could learn to be was

Not afraid of feeling this afraid.

Not ashamed of feeling this ashamed.

Not upset at feeling this upset.

Not distressed at feeling this distressed

Not overwhelmed at feeling this overwhelmed

Not hopeless at feeling this hopeless.

I could only listen to those parts of myself. To relax that hypervigilance. And be for them a gentle kind of company. To face it with them with that patient, quiet trust. And to those Strangers I would say, "I don't know what this is; I don't know what it is I'm feeling. I don't know what this is. But whatever it is, it is my life."

And I would begin to feel for it then the sweetness of what is mine. The sweetness of what is mine and not the Siren's.

My fear.

My anguish.

My hopelessness.

My distress.

The sweetness of what is mine, which can become the sweetness of what is mine to offer. The surprising pain of being human made holy by offering. Consecrated fear. Consecrated rage. Consecrated despair.

But that is all I knew. I didn't know what it all meant. I didn't know how it should direct me.

And I didn't need to know.

On the days when body, mind, and soul piled in, I simply began to make books out of scrap paper, string, and awls and hole punches. It was something I could do when I was miserable. I could make books. And saw that, as agonizing as it was, if I breathed Christ in and out, if I said "Lord, Lord" with every intake of breath, then, as agonizing as it could be, it was possible to bear each moment patiently and with Christ. Not understanding, but accepting with painful simplicity the things told to me by the Howling Boy, the Siren, the Body That Expected the World to End.

Feelings were such big, scary things.

I had trusted Christ with big, scary things. And was learning that Christ could be trusted with big, scary things.

I realized that I would do a lot of things, eat a lot of things, think a lot of things, to get rid of the John Who Feels This Way. That was what it meant to console myself, to get rid of the John Who Feels This Way.

But I couldn't get rid of him.

And I would say, again and again,

The John Who Feels This Way is welcome in my life.

The John Who Feels This Way is welcome in my life.

The John Who Feels This Way is welcome in my life.

And eventually something beautiful happened. The more I could resist the Siren, the more I could attend to the body, the more I could stand with the Howling Boy—the more of him I could look at and welcome—the fewer intrusive thoughts there were. The more relaxed my body became. The more it could be convinced to lose its hypervigilance. The more available I became to my own life.

CHRIST WILL COME AGAIN

At the Table with the Howling Boy

PART I

THE BIKE

GROWING UP, I NEVER BELIEVED I was a part of anything that was happening.

It was not an obvious thing. I was popular enough, well liked enough. When people were together and doing something, I could go and participate and maybe even enjoy myself but only while carrying a deeper assurance that I was not part of what was happening. Everyone was living their life and I was watching life being lived. I was not a part, it seemed, of what life was. It did not seem possible to become a part of things.

It has taken me a while to understand it was not even necessarily the world that had gotten rid of me. I did not even need the world to be mean to me. I had a brain that pushed, scolded, commanded, excused me from the world.

It could be said best with a moment from my childhood. It is one of my earliest memories.

One day, when I was five or six, my family was playing a game of Hungry Hungry Hippos. Everyone was piled in on the floor between the couches. And though I vividly remember wanting to play and join them, I also knew when I joined them that it wasn't what I wanted. I cannot remember what it was exactly that set me off, but something about it wasn't right, wasn't my game, my rules, what I wanted. The game was fun and everyone was nice, but something about it was still intolerable. Something about being there with my family and with that game just felt uncomfortable and wrong and I couldn't stand it. I had a brain that said, "No, this isn't right, no this isn't right." And I remember crying and storming off upset in ways I still can't explain.

And out there, away from the game, I was also crying because I was all alone and sad.

And I could not explain this to anybody: that to stay would make my mind cry, and to go would make my heart cry.

And I would go back and forth, crying that I wasn't a part of the game because it was like I had been abandoned and rejected, and crying when I was a part of the game because it was uncomfortable and just felt wrong.

I couldn't explain that something perfectly fine was actually intolerable.

There he was, even then, the Howling Boy fighting with a brain that is not like other brains, blind heart fighting stupidly, blindly with what his brain makes him feel. Believing the Siren that abuses him. Unable to cross the painful threshold back into his life. The unbearable dissatisfaction.

There were, of course, exceptions. Beautiful, clear, exceptions. Days when I seemed to cross some invisible threshold and find myself, somehow, beautifully and humbly a part of things. One of those moments is also one of my earliest memories.

Again when I was five or six, my parents took us to a creek of cold, clear water. I saw there was enough room between the boulders for a boy my size to put on his goggles, dip his body into cold, clear water, swim through the rocks, and look at all the fish. The water only went up to my waist, and so I could stand up, breathe in, and tell my mom that I had never been this happy in my entire life.

At that moment I felt no need to catch the fish or have them. The joy was in seeing them. The joy was getting to be where they were.

I knew, of course, that this wasn't my water, my creek, my fish. I was simply an honored guest at a moment I could have never created for myself. I knew then that in some way I had been anointed with a transfiguring Mercy called this time and this place and this water and these fish. And it was not something you could squeeze and grab at. It was something to be received while kneeling. It was sheer, unexpected gift. To be a part of things.

ON THE SAME VISIT WHERE, after a nap, I met the John in Whom Mercy Was Fulfilled (the John I would become, the John who could trust the Lord and pay attention), I told my mom I'd written a book, and written a lot of it on this visit. I could tell it moved her.

"It just all came out of you," she said, wise and eating biscuits in the recliner. "That's because when you're home you remember who you are."

I can't think of a visit that has meant more to me. I knew this trip was different because the thirteen-hour trip home—a long, winding journey through mountains of West Virginia, Kentucky, and ending in the suburbs of Tennessee—felt like being at home. I'd never felt that before, and I didn't know what to make of it.

I wrote in the morning and in the late afternoon, and when I took a break, I rode my dad's bike.

When I rode my dad's bike, I was captive to the sensation, as I drifted on my bike along old paths, that I was a pleasant ghost among the places that I'd been and the things that I'd done. The Past, for the first time in a long time, was not a bully or intruder. The Past was a gentle kind of company, an unexpected and accommodating friend. The Past was there to support me, to hold me in place. Not to hijack me, suck me out to sea.

I felt less real than the things I was remembering, felt that the things I remembered were on stage under bright lights and I was peeking behind the curtain. I felt like I was interrupting all the prior versions of myself, felt like they were being bothered by a ghost who needed to see them. That who I was now was less real than who I was then.

My dad, with the way his health is now, cannot go on these trips with me, and yet what I felt surrounded by as I drifted along was his long, sweet faithfulness on these trips, taking us on Saturdays, the trips getting longer and longer as we got older and older until the whole town was a place we loved by having ridden through it. Every hill, every tree, every trail, every old monument had a way of saying "Your dad was good to you."

And I found, then, moments that meant nothing to the ten-year-old living it were beautiful, tragic to the thirty-one-year-old remembering. All the beauty and grandeur that I should have had while living it I had now while remembering it.

Memory, come back to me.

John, come back to me.

I want to see you.

On those long bike rides, I was approached by all the previous versions of myself. And got to greet them: the John playing wallball in fifth grade, the John sledding down that hill when he was eleven, teenage John, moody and fishing. I saw they hadn't gone anywhere; they were still there to be remembered, and that they had time to walk up, to greet me and show me what they'd been doing, show me what they'd been up to.

And it was heart-achingly beautiful to find them there.

Come back to me.

Come back to me.

Come back to me.

I want to see you.

But there was, in all of this, in all of this trip, a John I'd meant to find. And finding him, I realized, was the purpose of the long bike rides. It was the pilgrimage I was on.

When you look back and try to remember how you became the person you've become, when you conduct a diligent search, what do you find?

The John who won't play Hungry Hungry Hippos, yes, but what else?

I know this: when I was seventeen something happened. Something definitely happened.

Finishing high school, after a disappointing senior year of high-school basketball, I remember at first shooting hoops with everyone on the team after class, then when it was time to run sprints, realizing I didn't have to.

Not having to run sprints used to mean: "I don't have to run sprints." Now it meant: "You don't belong here. You're not wanted here." I wasn't a part of next year's team. Senior year had ended. I'd been pretty good at rebounding and passing, but that was all I'd been pretty good at. I hadn't done terrible, and I hadn't done well.

A few weeks earlier, I'd given my last performance playing trumpet. There was no reason to be at band practice. I used to hate band practice. But now not having to go to band practice meant I was unwanted.

I don't think I was particularly sad about it, and I definitely wasn't miserable. There was just a feeling of drift. I no longer felt placed.

I remember, with nothing to do after school, I would go home early. And when I got home, I would go walking for hours. And I remember thinking many things then, on those long walks I took as a seventeen-year-old boy that I retrace now as a thirty-one-year old on my dad's bike. I don't remember what I was particularly thinking on those long walks. I only remember that it was then that thinking itself became a hobby. The place where I built mansions for myself. Where I learned my thoughts were the company I would keep, that they were more interesting and trustworthy and would bless me more than the few friends I had and the few attempts I had made at having more friends.

I knew how to be quiet and how to be funny, but it would take many years to learn what a friendship was. And what it was like to be with people. And by then maybe some kind of damage was already done.

I would walk around listening to Bob Dylan. His was the voice that acquainted me with how to be lonely. I simply did not know, until I'd heard Bob Dylan play the guitar and sing terribly, that you could say the things that he said in the way he said them. And to this day, his song "Mr. Tambourine Man" is still what loneliness sounds like to me, or to put it differently, what it's like to get used to being lonely. Its power and its privilege and its pull and its terror.

But that John, the seventeen-year-old John wandering in and out of old trails and sidewalks and listening to Bob Dylan, as much as I love him, has made a bad decision. He has made the decision to be by himself. The few group things he went on he felt either that he was pitied or that he was there to make people laugh. He has decided it isn't worth trying to be something else to other people. And to prefer being by himself.

But there was a price for him to pay. And I can remember one moment where he paid for it.

In the interim between finishing high school and graduating high school—again, one of those strange days when there was very little to be done—that John goes with his dad to a church basketball game, knowing his dad doesn't make a lot of friends and John will be his only company. And his dad, when he gets to the game, is asked to be the coach and so moves to the seats by the players. And somehow John feels rejected, left by his dad. That his dad has turned his face from him. And with it feels so keenly humiliated. And even though he's seventeen and going to go to a great school and is graduating valedictorian, something about his dad leaving him makes him feel humiliated in a way he can't explain and maybe even now I can't explain for him.

When that John was a child and his father rode bikes with him, his father got so far ahead that John couldn't keep up and his dad wouldn't look back to see if John was behind him, and John—indulging in some kind of fit of self-pity so that he would, on purpose, feel even more humiliated—didn't say anything to slow his dad down and just kept on falling farther and farther behind.

When that John was twelve he was on a ski trip with people he didn't know well and was too slow on his skis, and everyone but his dad, who was chaperoning, went ahead, and the humiliation and the unbearable dissatisfaction and the keen feeling of rejection almost had a sweetness to it that he still can't get over and indulges now when he's seventeen and at this basketball game, and so his seventeen-year-old self goes outside and walks around a nearby park and just starts crying as the evening sets in. And this seventeen-year-old John who has decided to be alone is crying now. And worst of all, he can't tell you why. He doesn't have the words I have for him now, the understanding I have for him now, grown man that I now am, and with all the education and experience I can put toward saying it for him.

And his dad, after the game, doesn't understand why his grown six-foot-seven, near-handsome, valedictorian middle son is crying in a park for no reason.

And I don't, except that it's about being alone, its privilege and its sweetness and its terror and its power, and when it began and how deep must it go because I feel it still when I dream, the dream where I can't explain something that's very important to people I love, those dreams where I'm crying and I don't know why and then in the dream I frighten myself and the people in my life by hitting the wall again and again and again. With all that unbearable dissatisfaction.

And why?

Why?

Why?

Because I am scared.

Because I am not wanted.

Because the world is not as I would have it.

CHRIST WILL COME AGAIN

At the Table with the Howling Boy

PART II
THE CABIN

IT GOT TO THE POINT in my recovery where I felt good enough, I thought, to travel. And so my wife and I did.

It was our five-year anniversary. My wife and I were to go on a trip to the mountains. I was excited about the trip but nervous. I was nervous it would ruin the Rhythm that had become my life. My life of coffee shops and care homes and biking around places. The life that made me feel placed.

Travel was hard. It still is. With travel come transitions, thresholds, logistics, complications, disorientation, agitation, unrest. A feeling of being unsettled. All very normal human things exploited and magnified by the Siren so that it can say,

Something's wrong.

Something's intolerable.

Something bad is going to happen.

Our car wound through the mountains. We came to a clearing in the trees, and I was struck. I knew that what I was looking at was big and beautiful mountains but did not feel as though I was looking at them but that I was confronted by them. I felt like they saw me first and laughed.

These mountains. We had found a cabin, some intimate, vulnerable perch half an hour up a steep and windy gravel road, a little cabin up in the woods where we would look at those mountains for three days.

I could not put into words what it felt like to have my life put in front of that kind of unexpected sovereignty. To feel placed by mountains, some things in this world so haunting and obvious that just by looking at them you feel you have been corrected, been made small, not by self-hatred but by the need to be silent. You have become a servant and guest by looking at them.

Rats came to live with me that weekend, all of them it seemed, the greatest hits chewing mildly on my face. The Siren came to me with all its horrors, came to feast on my unrest, agitation, transition. But it was not just that.

OCD made me afraid, more often than other things, of the tenderness, the vulnerability, of households, of ordinary time with people I love. It is the most embarrassing thing about having this mental illness. It did not even need a particular trigger. It was an amorphous dread, a free-floating sense of impending doom, landing softly in the background of every moment I was in.

In telling people what it's like to have OCD, I often tell them to imagine they had a friend who has seen every moment of their life, who walked every step with them. Who shared all of the tenderness and mystery of it.

And to imagine that friend suddenly began to lie and torture you.

The Siren came alive speaking, as it always did, in tones both intimate and catastrophic. Turning the world into what it isn't. Telling me things that were very ugly, very secret, very tender. With an urgency and a condemnation that was not possible. With an excruciating, impossible plausibility. Filling me with that kind of dumbstruck, awe-filled dread: the unique devastation of the disorder.

I was there, vulnerable as I ever was. And with the Strangers I carried with me, the Siren prone to abusing the Howling Boy, and the Howling Boy prone to believing the Siren. And the body in terror at both.

And the urges. All the powerful urges I used to not have to feel what I was feeling.

John, know for sure.

John, figure it out.

John, defend yourself.

John, make it right.

And I felt so immaculately frail. So compromised. I was a nerve ending. So undeniably implicated in my own great, crying, and shivering exposure to my own body, mind, and soul.

I would do almost anything to not feel this way.

But I had to.

And without a pool or a schedule or a coffee shop or a care home or friends, all I had was this view of the mountains. The mountains had their own two tones, their own two voices, that tenderness and severity.

First, the severity, their solemn authority: they would continue, and I would not. Their majesty and scale. I would be condemned by time and circumstance. They would not.

Second, their tenderness: my wife and me hidden in them. Us frail birds hung up on a perch. The tenderness, the intimacy, of somehow being the one they were protecting up here.

Severe because I felt tiny; intimate because I, specifically, was the one made to feel tiny. A humility that gave me back to myself.

I looked around the cabin. I looked at my wife. Trying to understand our remarkable frailty as a sweetness rather than as condemnation. As part of my life again rather than an indictment of it: to not be afraid but to instead be nourished by the fact that we were really and truly on this cliff, just hanging there. In the middle of nowhere. Helpless and blessed. This frailty the OCD always managed to pick on.

This frailty that always felt intolerable, wrong, perilous.

This uncertainty that always felt intolerable, wrong, perilous.

This tenderness that always felt intolerable, wrong, perilous.

This helplessness that always felt intolerable, wrong, perilous.

The way OCD would seize every awkward and nightmarish possibility and say it would happen, it would definitely happen, it would absolutely definitely happen.

That excruciating, urgent way it said, "John, something is wrong, something is intolerable, something bad is about to happen, you need to do something to be okay."

And the pain, that ongoing everyday experience still so fresh, still there even after Jesus died for you and after Jesus has told you again and again that He died to save you. This kind of pain: to be playing a board game with your wife in that cabin, eating steaks you cooked together, and for your wife to notice something's wrong with you and for you to simply be too embarrassed to tell her. Because what's wrong is that you had an intrusive thought and now you're worried it might come true.

This thing that has made you afraid of vacations.

The Siren. The Bully. The Accuser.

But when I stared at the mountains it got quiet in my heart and I think I understood something else: creation could not hold a candle to re-creation. Even mountains stood solemn at the solemnity of the cross.

That Word. That death. The anointing. Who He is and who I am. That patient, quiet understanding.

The tenderness found in this little perch within these solemn mountains was nothing to the tenderness of that death. When God bent His heart toward our littleness.

That Word. That death. The anointing. That patient, quiet understanding.

The questions of my heart were laid bare, again, before Jesus and the mountains:

"When will I be sane and honored?"

"When would I be okay?"

"Would I ever be okay?"

"Would I ever be okay?"

It was the question that framed all of my life in the Realm of Ceaseless Cognition. I still held on to a bargain in the dark left corner of my heart—I would let Jesus Christ be my Lord and Savior if He kept me out of the psych ward.

I was mad the Lord would not guarantee it. I thought I deserved that much. But the Lord knew, knew the bargain, the request, was a part of the vicious regime that was killing me. The hardness of my heart known as Life as I Would Have It.

"Will I be okay?"

I stared at the mountains longer and longer. Something about mountains makes it easier to imagine Christ's return. To imagine him coming up over them to see you and to be seen by you.

"When Christ who is your life appears, you will appear with Him in glory."

"You have my life," Christ seemed to say by having me look at mountains. By turning my heart toward mountains. Where it seemed like Christ coming back was a real thing.

"You have my life. And the only thing that matters is my life. But you do not have it by argument, by feeling, by effort, by circumstance. You can have all of it. And it's the only real life there is. But you only have it by trust and frailty."

I was here, and this was a vulnerable place. And it was not my job to be invulnerable. It was my job to be led. To be led by the Christ I could depend on toward my dependence on Christ. And led to what? Fulfilled by what?

An intrusive thought popped up, something random, something stupid, something catastrophic, something that could possibly happen and would never happen. I began to argue with it so I would feel better. I began to go into my head to make it right. I began to go into one of the doors in the long hallways of my mind and make sure it wouldn't happen.

I began to console myself.

What will happen if I am not there to defend myself? If I am not here to argue my case? If I am not there to make it right?

These two things that would always contend in my heart: the fear of the Lord, by which my life was Christ's, and the desire to know for sure, by which my life was mine.

I kept looking at the mountains. They seemed to hold court with silence. To make it a verdict over all of us. The quiet in the mountains that squeezed out my eyes. I knew what it meant.

It meant there was no argument left.

No defense left.

There was a John who could hear the gospel and look at mountains, and a John who could not. That was all there was. There were few things here: my wife, these mountains, and the death of the Son of God. And that patient, quiet understanding. Nothing more beautiful and harrowing than having to become that patient, quiet understanding.

I knew, then, what intrusive thoughts were, what these horrible uncomfortable feelings were. What OCD was meant to be.

Because I could not fix them, because I could not make them go away, they could only be something I trusted Christ with, the deepening of my trust in Christ, a time of patience waiting on the Mercy offered in the gospel.

These nightmares were the place where I stood in greatest need to not think and not act and not worry. They were my vulnerability; they were a place of deliverance, of waiting. Intrusive thoughts were an instruction in Mercy.

Shame and fear and unbearable dissatisfaction were an instruction in Mercy. They were too powerful to be anything else, too painful and powerful to be anything I could handle. They were only the revelation of who Christ would have to be. They could only be overcome by Christ. They could only be overcome by hearing. By being spoken to. By that patient, quiet understanding.

Only overcome by trust.

An instruction in Mercy. I could only stand firm while He clothed the shame, cast out the fear, endured My Affliction, overturned the verdict, and buried the Hardness of the Heart.

My wife came outside, sat on the porch with me. She was wearing a new shirt.

"Maybe she's a wildflower," it said.

"There's my wildflower," I said. My wildflower.

The Howling Boy interjected:

"When will I ever be sane and honored?"

"When will I be okay?"

The questions that had made my life lonely and about me.

I knew as long as I honored those questions, I would not have my wife.

My wife and I had argued a few years before. "I feel like I have to compete for attention with your interior life," she'd said. "I feel like I'm never as interesting as what's going on in your head."

She wasn't being mean, I realized, months later. She was being vulnerable and correct.

"When will I be okay?"

I felt myself giving the question up.

You cannot make sure you're okay.

You can only trust you're okay.

I had not been asked to carry the burden of knowing for sure. Only the burden of hearing and of prayer and of offering: to let the Lord have it His way, to live without knowing if I'd get better, to live without knowing for sure if I'd end up back in a psych ward, to stand there and be with my wife and feel awful because there were things that were more important than feeling better. And my wife was one of them. To finally begin to offer myself to her.

My thoughts and feelings might never return to me as consolation again. I would have to make my life about something else. I would have to make my life about paying attention. To live simply and vulnerably with Christ, so that I might learn to pay attention. To be delivered, moment by moment, from my dependence on myself so that I might gradually be able to pay attention.

What did I need to be okay?

What did I need to be okay?

Trust.

A trust that could be rescued by hearing. So that I could trust in Christ.

A trust that could then be led through prayer.

So I could trust Christ with things.

That could then be fulfilled in offering. So I could entrust myself to others.

And this was what I could offer. My attention. My company.

I would define getting better as being able to see my wife.

To be able to really see her, really enjoy her, really serve her.

To be present with my wife as an offering to Christ. To depend on Christ by paying attention. To depend on Christ by risking paying attention.

I saw then that my attention was not just something taken from me and scattered by my brain. The trust that bore the secret of who I was could be fulfilled by my attention. My trust and attention: the two things I could give, could intend to give. The two things that would bear the secret of who I was.

I could always have what things are.

If my thoughts did not count her as precious.

If my feelings did not regard her as precious.

By trust and attention I could have my wife as precious.

With an attention that was painful and transfiguring. That turns us into servants and guests.

My attention could be pulled out of that tangled ball of yarn in my mind, be made to rest on something in this world like a sheer garment, to neither distort nor cloak it but to hallow it. To make it sacred unto the Lord. With that patient, quiet understanding. With all that painful simplicity. With those few intentions.

It could be done with the trust I had in Christ.

With that trust in Christ, and its prosaic expression through an Ordinary Life of Regular Worship, I could head somewhere, could embark on the greatest adventure.

To be delivered from my compulsions through hearing.

To accept what I am feeling in prayer.

And to be where I am by offering.

To be in this world. To arrive back here. To expect that I can become a part of things.

Because the Lord is coming back for this world and not for any other. And for these people and not for any other. And if it is, finally, His world and His people, then maybe I will, finally, serve it and serve them. Serve the world that will not be changed by my effort or sorrow but by His return, a return that will finally gather and fulfill and forgive His people and set a Table for them.

A Table where they are seen.

A Table where they are fed.

A Table where they can pay attention.

I could serve that table and serve now, and serve well: made glad, small, trusting, loved, peripheral. Not the center of the Table, not the feast, not the banquet. But that servant over there, in the corner, putting the food in front of his wife, putting the food in front of the schizophrenics. Finally able to see them. Happy to just be there. Neither god nor Stranger. Servant and guest. Finally a person in a place. A part of things.

"When will I be okay?"

I felt myself giving the question up.

And felt, for the first time in a long time, perfectly capable of flirting with my wife. I found myself stunned, again, by her grace and humor. She joked, she taunted. This woman who would read me psalms and then make fun of me like this!

There is a moment people with OCD find. The moment your brain releases you from its terrors, and you find yourself not simply less worried, but having crossed a threshold back into your life, having walked, as it were, into a clearing. You're not less worried about something—you wonder why you were worried at all, why things so obviously stupid and impossible had such a hold on you. You find yourself silly and relieved. I found myself, then, welcomed back into the tenderness and frailty of my own life. Taking a seat at the table. Not as someone in charge of it by worry, but in awe of it by fear and thanksgiving and grace and service.

And one day later I took a pen and paper, and to the Howling Boy I wrote this letter:

Dear Howling Boy,

I'm sorry, buddy. I'm sorry I didn't listen to you. I'm sorry I spent so much time making you go away. I'm sorry I didn't recognize you behind the hieroglyphics of those intrusive thoughts.

They frightened me so much.

I'm sorry I didn't listen to you. I'm sorry that I tried to get rid of you. I'm sorry you frightened me so much.

I'm sorry I didn't listen when you said you weren't safe, you weren't wanted, and too much had already been taken.

Please, come to the Table I've found. There is more here than we ever knew. Christ Himself has met us here.

And if you will not come, may the good Lord find you, in the places you wander and in the places where you scream and punch walls in my dreams and in the places where you hide. May the good Lord find you and take you gently by the hand and lead you here.

Come back to me.

I would like to see you.

I will anoint you with the oil of gladness.

I will anoint you with the oil of gladness.

CHRIST WILL COME AGAIN

At the Table with the Howling Boy

PART III
THE BEACH

ABOUT THE TIME I WAS finishing this book, I went to the beach with my family. And I felt every lesson I learned over these last three years I learned again, all at once, in that one week. It was harrowing, ugly, beautiful, transfiguring.

Usually when I go off somewhere for a while, I carry a stack of books with me. It would be unthinkable to bring nothing on vacation. But this time, for the first time, I felt I could.

I packed only a Bible.

I felt the Lord say, for this vacation, I would need less. That, maybe for the rest of my life, I would need less. Would always need less.

Just a week prior I had been given, by my wife, the biggest compliment yet in my recovery.

She said, "It seems like you need less to be okay."

It felt good to hear that.

But it was going to be a hard week.

My wife had to hang back and run a summer camp. Coming on vacation without her, I felt adrift.

In the place where we'd lived there were many messy relationships. It was not clear what to do with them. I came on this vacation with those relationships unresolved.

In the place where we lived there was a house we wanted. But we just couldn't seem to get together the paperwork we needed to make the offer in time. I came on this vacation without knowing if we'd get the house.

There were things at work that simply weren't coming together. I couldn't make them right before coming on vacation.

On vacation, I brought those things with me. A head full of What Should Happen, a body anticipating What Could Happen.

I wanted to figure those relationships out.

I wanted to make sure we got the house.

I wanted to make things at work right.

But on that vacation, there was, clearly, no way to. And with no way to make things right, I was left with

The urge to figure things out.

The urge to make sure.

The urge to make things right.

Without any way to console myself, to fix it, I was simply left with what was going on in me. And it was intense, and it was uncomfortable. A lot of fear, a lot of shame, and the desire to somehow, someway, console myself. To reach out for something that would make me feel okay.

I wanted above all to reach out for narrative, to hold on to some story.

And the Lord made it clear:

You're going to have to be okay without it.

Without any consolation or story, I found myself not only irritated but met with other desires, other urges. It turns out I had compulsions in my head (make sure, figure out, make right) as well as compulsions in the world:

To eat.

To stare.

To check things.

To avoid.

To be alone.

Though I did not do them, I was still left with the tremendous urge to. They came upon me with a surprising ferocity. And with them the fear that I would be overthrown by the hardness of my own heart. I would be overthrown by what I would do to be okay.

All those powerful things kept leaping out of me.

I took lots of long walks to get myself all good and sorted out.

But on those long walks with Scripture and prayer I was not rescued from the thoughts and feelings and urges, but only the trust I had in them.

Perhaps I've said that before.

The ocean that week was strong and peculiarly treacherous: the waves were choppy and obvious, there was a riptide invisible to the eye that had already drowned four people that summer.

More than once I had to drag my mama back when I saw it sucking her out to the horizon.

It was, I thought, the perfect metaphor. The waves—circumstances beyond control, the things that happen to us. But also—powerful and invisible—the riptide, the invisible downward pull of a mental illness that will suck you out to sea while just a moment ago you were laughing and playing in the sea with everyone else. And with it also the dark pull of self, the hidden, inexorable pull of that vicious regime called Life as I Would Have It. The dark pull of What I Would Do to Be Okay.

I looked at the ocean. Its beauty and its terror. The ocean had no idea it was going to be a metaphor in my book.

THE WATER WAS TREACHEROUS.

And yet every day we went out into the water.

We were, my family and I, strangely confident people.

My nephew was getting happily demolished by the shallow waves.

What was remarkable to show him, and to rediscover for myself, is that, even with those tremendous forces of the sea, an eight-year-old and his thirty-two-year-old uncle got to have a relationship to it. We could change our relationship to it.

I showed him how to check your stance as a big wave comes in, how to make yourself small and dive under the wave so that it doesn't demolish you. And I myself remembered how to check my stance.

And in the water, I felt the choppy waves and the undertow. I thought, again, of myself. Of the tremendous pull of the Siren. The terror of the body. The howl of the soul's despair. All the pain, confusion, and dissatisfaction.

I let it pull on me. I let it be what it was—grief, a longing, an urgency. A temptation. But I let that be all that it was.

But I also saw, wonder of wonders, that though it pulled, I had not been handed over. I had the Spirit-led power of simple renunciation. I was not taken out to sea. And though I was tempted, though I was howling, though I was what I was, I was still here, and I was not afraid, and I was not ashamed.

I had a place to stand. An ability to overcome by not being overcome.

It's not our desires that kill us. It's the trust we have in them.

I was not moved because I had found my stance. Because that is what a life with Christ is, a stance. A peculiar and deepening stance. A stance found with Christ, and a Christ found by hearing, through prayer, in offering. A peculiar stance found in peculiar ways. But a stance nonetheless. A way to hold on to the Christ who holds on to me. A way to stand firm and be led while He clothes the shame, casts out the fear, endures every affliction, bears all history, mends all brokenness, overturns all accusation, and buries the hardness of heart. And does this by His Word.

And when I was done in the water, I went back out to my family. And found, miracle of miracles, that I could be an uncle to my nephews, a son to my father and to my mother. I could, somehow, slowly but surely point myself to what I had decided was meaningful. And to stay there longer and longer, to deepen and extend my time on the other side of the glass. To set up camp in what I had decided was meaningful. Which was, more often than not, just listening, just being there and helping out. Being available. Being part of things.

On the last day, my youngest nephew took his first steps into the ocean, and I was there, pretending I was a giant crab coming after him. In between him running out and in, it was just me and the waves.

My dad came and stood beside me.

I remembered—all over again and yet in some fresh way—that my dad was deeply kind and gentle, that I loved him. Because I did.

This was his seventieth-birthday trip. We'd spent summers growing up at the beach. We were finally back at the beach. Doing the things we had done at the beach as if we had never stopped doing them: sandcastles, playing catch, body surfing. As if there were no gap between then and now.

And now we had passed down some of that tradition to my nephews. I had been able to be an uncle. To listen to them, to show them things. I had been able to really be there.

And rather than look back at this moment in nostalgia later, I was able to cry as it was happening.

And I wept.

I wept because my dad is old now and not that long ago he wasn't.

And I wept because it was my life that was beautiful and precious and passing before my eyes and it was my life that was finally happening to me.

The Lord had not committed Himself to my plans. He had committed Himself to my freedom.

And there I was, delivered in the churning water.

I had arrived on the other side of the glass that had separated me from my life.

And I stayed there, crying, as long as I could.

SCRIPTURE REFERENCES